HEALTH AND INCARCERATION

A Workshop Summary

Amy Smith, *Rapporteur*

Committee on Causes and Consequences of High Rates of Incarceration

Committee on Law and Justice
Division of Behavioral and Social Sciences and Education

Board on the Health of Select Populations
Institute of Medicine

NATIONAL RESEARCH COUNCIL AND
INSTITUTE OF MEDICINE
OF THE NATIONAL ACADEMIES

THE NATIONAL ACADEMIES PRESS
Washington, D.C.
www.nap.edu

THE NATIONAL ACADEMIES PRESS   500 Fifth Street, NW   Washington, DC 20001

NOTICE: The project that is the subject of this report was approved by the Governing Board of the National Research Council, whose members are drawn from the councils of the National Academy of Sciences, the National Academy of Engineering, and the Institute of Medicine. The members of the committee responsible for the report were chosen for their special competences and with regard for appropriate balance.

This study was supported by Grant No. 70863 from the Robert Wood Johnson Foundation, Grant No. 99472-0 from the John D. and Catherine T. MacArthur Foundation, and Grant No. 2011-DJ-BX-2029 from the National Institute of Justice. Any opinions, findings, conclusions, or recommendations expressed in this publication are those of the author(s) and do not necessarily reflect the views of the organizations or agencies that provided support for the project.

International Standard Book Number-13:   978-0-309-28768-5
International Standard Book Number-10:   0-309-28768-5

Additional copies of this report are available from the National Academies Press, 500 Fifth Street, NW, Keck 360, Washington, DC 20001; (800) 624-6242 or (202) 334-3313; http://www.nap.edu.

Copyright 2013 by the National Academy of Sciences. All rights reserved.

Printed in the United States of America

Suggested citation: National Research Council and Institute of Medicine. (2013). *Health and Incarceration: A Workshop Summary.* A. Smith, Rapporteur. Committee on Law and Justice, Division of Behavioral and Social Sciences and Education and Board on the Health of Select Populations, Institute of Medicine. Washington, DC: The National Academies Press.

THE NATIONAL ACADEMIES
Advisers to the Nation on Science, Engineering, and Medicine

The **National Academy of Sciences** is a private, nonprofit, self-perpetuating society of distinguished scholars engaged in scientific and engineering research, dedicated to the furtherance of science and technology and to their use for the general welfare. Upon the authority of the charter granted to it by the Congress in 1863, the Academy has a mandate that requires it to advise the federal government on scientific and technical matters. Dr. Ralph J. Cicerone is president of the National Academy of Sciences.

The **National Academy of Engineering** was established in 1964, under the charter of the National Academy of Sciences, as a parallel organization of outstanding engineers. It is autonomous in its administration and in the selection of its members, sharing with the National Academy of Sciences the responsibility for advising the federal government. The National Academy of Engineering also sponsors engineering programs aimed at meeting national needs, encourages education and research, and recognizes the superior achievements of engineers. Dr. C. D. Mote, Jr., is president of the National Academy of Engineering.

The **Institute of Medicine** was established in 1970 by the National Academy of Sciences to secure the services of eminent members of appropriate professions in the examination of policy matters pertaining to the health of the public. The Institute acts under the responsibility given to the National Academy of Sciences by its congressional charter to be an adviser to the federal government and, upon its own initiative, to identify issues of medical care, research, and education. Dr. Harvey V. Fineberg is president of the Institute of Medicine.

The **National Research Council** was organized by the National Academy of Sciences in 1916 to associate the broad community of science and technology with the Academy's purposes of furthering knowledge and advising the federal government. Functioning in accordance with general policies determined by the Academy, the Council has become the principal operating agency of both the National Academy of Sciences and the National Academy of Engineering in providing services to the government, the public, and the scientific and engineering communities. The Council is administered jointly by both Academies and the Institute of Medicine. Dr. Ralph J. Cicerone and Dr. C. D. Mote, Jr., are chair and vice chair, respectively, of the National Research Council.

www.national-academies.org

COMMITTEE ON CAUSES AND CONSEQUENCES OF HIGH RATES OF INCARCERATION

JEREMY TRAVIS (*Chair*), John Jay College of Criminal Justice, City University of New York
BRUCE WESTERN (*Vice Chair*), Department of Sociology and the Malcolm Wiener Center for Social Policy at the Harvard University Kennedy School of Government
JEFFREY BEARD, California Department of Corrections and Rehabilitation
ROBERT D. CRUTCHFIELD, Department of Sociology, University of Washington
TONY FABELO, Council of State Governments Justice Center
MARIE GOTTSCHALK, Department of Political Science, University of Pennsylvania
CRAIG HANEY, Department of Psychology, Graduate Program in Social Psychology, and Program in Legal Studies, University of California, Santa Cruz
RICHARDO H. HINOJOSA, U.S. District Court, Southern District of Texas
GLENN C. LOURY, Department of Economics, Brown University
SARA S. McLANAHAN, Department of Sociology and Public Affairs, Princeton University
LAWRENCE M. MEAD, Department of Politics and Public Policy, New York University
KHALIL GIBRAN MUHAMMAD, Schomburg Center for Research in Black Culture, New York Public Library
DANIEL S. NAGIN, Department of Public Policy and Statistics, Carnegie Mellon University
DEVAH PAGER, Department of Sociology and the Joint Degree Program in Social Policy, Princeton University
ANNE MORRISON PIEHL, Department of Economics and Program in Criminal Justice, Rutgers University
JOSIAH D. RICH, Department of Medicine and Epidemiology, Warren Alpert Medical School of Brown University, and the Center for Prisoner Health and Human Rights at the Miriam Hospital Immunology Center
ROBERT J. SAMPSON, Department of Sociology, Harvard University
HEATHER ANN THOMPSON, Department of History, Temple University
MICHAEL TONRY, University of Minnesota Law School
AVELARDO VALDEZ, School of Social Work, University of Southern California

STEVE REDBURN, *Study Director*
MALAY MAJMUNDAR, *Senior Program Officer*
JULIE SCHUCK, *Senior Program Associate*
BARBARA BOYD, *Administrative Coordinator*

COMMITTEE ON LAW AND JUSTICE
2013

JEREMY TRAVIS (*Chair*), John Jay College of Criminal Justice, City University of New York

RUTH D. PETERSON (*Vice Chair*), Department of Sociology, Ohio State University

CARL C. BELL, Community Mental Health Council, Inc.

JOHN J. DONOHUE III, Stanford Law School

MARK A.R. KLEIMAN, Department of Public Policy, University of California, Los Angeles

GARY LAFREE, Department of Criminology and Criminal Justice, University of Maryland, College Park

JANET L. LAURITSEN, Department of Criminology and Criminal Justice, University of Missouri

GLENN LOURY, Department of Economics, Brown University

CHARLES F. MANSKI, Department of Economics, Northwestern University

DANIEL S. NAGIN, Department of Public Policy and Statistics, Carnegie Mellon University

ANNE MORRISON PIEHL, Department of Economics and Program in Criminal Justice, Rutgers University

DANIEL B. PRIETO, Public Sector Strategy and Innovation, IBM Global Business Services, Washington, DC

DAVID WEISBURD, Center for Evidence-Based Crime Policy, George Mason University

PAUL K. WORMELI, Integrated Justice Information Systems, Ashburn, VA

CATHY SPATZ WIDOM, Psychology Department, John Jay College of Criminal Justice, City University of New York

ARLENE LEE, *Director*

BOARD ON THE HEALTH OF SELECT POPULATIONS
2013

DAN G. BLAZER (*Chair*), Duke University Medical Center
KATHLEEN BRADY, Department of Psychiatry and Behavioral Sciences, Medical University of South Carolina
JOHN C.S. BREITNER, Department of Psychiatry, McGill University, Montreal, Quebec, Canada
MICHAEL L. COWAN, Broadlands, VA
WALTER R. FRONTERA, Vanderbilt University School of Medicine and Vanderbilt University Medical Center
GREGORY C. GRAY, Department of Environmental and Global Health and Department of Infectious Diseases and Pathology, University of Florida, Gainesville
KURT KROENKE, Department of Medicine, Indiana University School of Medicine
JANICE L. KRUPNICK, Department of Psychiatry, Georgetown University School of Medicine
STANLEY M. LEMON, Department of Medicine and Microbiology and Immunology Inflammatory Diseases Institute, University of North Carolina at Chapel Hill
VICKIE M. MAYS, Department of Psychology, University of California, Los Angeles, Fielding School of Public Health
M. JEANNE MIRANDA, Center for Health Services and Society, University of California, Los Angeles
FRANCES M. MURPHY, Sigma Health Consulting, LLC, Silver Spring, MD
KENNETH OLDEN, National Center for Environmental Assessment and Human Health Risk Assessment Research Program, Environmental Protection Agency
MICHAEL D. PARKINSON, UPMC Health Plan and WorkPartners, Pittsburgh, PA
JENNIFER D. PECK, Department of Biostatistics and Epidemiology, University of Oklahoma Health Sciences Center
CAROL K. REDMOND, Department of Public Health, University of Pittsburgh
GRACE S. ROZYCKI, Emory University School of Medicine/Grady Memorial Hospital
GEORGE W. RUTHERFORD, Department of Epidemiology, University of California, San Francisco School of Medicine
MURRAY B. STEIN, Department of Psychiatry and Family and Preventive Medicine, University of California, San Diego

FREDERICK (RICK) ERDTMANN, *Director*

Preface

Over the past four decades, the rate of incarceration in the United States has skyrocketed to unprecedented heights, both historically and in comparison to that of other developed nations. At far higher rates than the general population, those in or entering U.S. jails and prisons are prone to many health problems. This is a problem not just for them, but also for the communities from which they come and to which, in nearly all cases, they will return.

A changing policy environment calls for a fresh look at the connections between health and incarceration. Costs of providing care to prisoners are rising, driven partly by an aging of that population. Fiscal pressures, litigation, and judicial oversight are pushing states to look for alternatives that better meet health needs of the incarcerated. The Patient Protection and Affordable Care Act (ACA), in addition to insuring millions of previously uninsured people, creates specific new opportunities to ensure continuity of medical coverage and care when prisoners are released.

On December 5, 2012, the Committee on Law and Justice of the National Research Council (NRC) and the Board on Health and Select Populations of the Institute of Medicine (IOM) sponsored a workshop on health and incarceration that brought together leading academic and practicing experts to review what is known about these health issues and what appear to be the best opportunities to improve healthcare for those who are now or will be incarcerated. The workshop was designed as a roundtable with brief presentations from 16 experts and time for group discussion.

The purpose of the workshop was to inform a current consensus study by the NRC Committee on Causes and Consequences of High Rates of Incarceration. In addition, participants hoped that a stand-alone document of the workshop proceedings could educate the healthcare and policy communities and provide a platform for visions of how the world of incarceration health can be a better place. I thank the Robert Wood Johnson Foundation for the generous support to enable this publication. This summary provides an objective report of what occurred at the workshop, drawing on views presented by individual participants and focusing on the possibilities for improving the health of incarcerated and formerly incarcerated populations and implications of the implementation of the ACA on public health.

As the vice chair of the committee that co-organized the workshop, I extend our thanks, first to committee member Josiah (Jody) Rich, Department of Medicine and Epidemiology, Warren Alpert Medical School of Brown University, and the Center for Prisoner Health and Human Rights at the Miriam Hospital Immunology Center, for his key role in identifying the expert participants and moderating the event. The success of the workshop was a result of a talented and thoughtful group who gave generously of their knowledge and time, whom we thank: Scott Allen, University of California, Riverside; Redonna Chandler, National Institute on Drug Abuse; Jennifer Clarke, Brown University Medical Center; Jamie Fellner, Human Rights Watch; Robert Greifinger, John Jay College of Criminal Justice, City University of New York; Newton Kendig, Federal Bureau of Prisons; Marc Mauer, The Sentencing Project; Fred Osher, Council of State Governments; Steven Rosenberg, Community Oriented Correctional Health Services; Faye Taxman, George Mason University; Emily Wang, Yale University; Christopher Wildeman, Yale University; and Brie Williams, University of California, San Francisco. In addition, my fellow committee member, Craig Haney, University of California, Santa Cruz, joined Jody Rich and me at the workshop.

I also thank Steve Redburn, study director for the committee, and Rick Erdtmann, director of IOM's Board on Health and Select Populations, for their ongoing consultation in preparation for the workshop. Barbara Boyd and Julie Schuck from the NRC's Committee on Law and Justice also provided valuable support to the workshop and production of the workshop summary. I also thank the executive office reports staff of the Division of Behavioral and Social Sciences and Education, especially Eugenia Grohman, who provided consultation with staff and the rapporteur on the writing and editing of this summary; Kirsten Sampson

Snyder, who managed the report review process; and Yvonne Wise, who managed the production process.

Finally, I thank our rapporteur, Amy Smith, who did a wonderful job capturing the many visions presented at the workshop.

This report has been reviewed in draft form by individuals chosen for their diverse perspectives and technical expertise, in accordance with procedures approved by the NRC's Report Review Committee. The purpose of this independent review is to provide candid and critical comments that will assist the institution in making its published report as sound as possible and to ensure that the report meets institutional standards for objectivity, evidence, and responsiveness to the study charge. The review comments and draft manuscript remain confidential to protect the integrity of the deliberative process. We thank the following individuals for their review of this report: Ingrid Binswanger, Primary Care Residency Research, School of Medicine, University of Colorado, Denver; Josiah D. Rich, Department of Medicine and Epidemiology, Warren Alpert Medical School of Brown University, and the Center for Prisoner Health and Human Rights at the Miriam Hospital Immunology Center; Emily Wang, General Internal Medicine, Yale School of Medicine; Brie Williams, Division of Geriatrics, University of California, San Francisco; and Lester N. Wright, Discipline of Public Health, University of Adelaide.

Although the reviewers listed above provided many constructive comments and suggestions, they were not asked to endorse the content of the report nor did they see the final draft of the report before its release. The review of this report was overseen by Philip J. Cook, Sanford School of Public Policy, Duke University. Appointed by the NRC, he was responsible for making certain that an independent examination of this report was carried out in accordance with institutional procedures and that all review comments were carefully considered. Responsibility for the final content of this report rests entirely with the author and the institution.

Bruce Western, *Vice Chair*
Committee on Causes and Consequences of
High Rates of Incarceration

Contents

INTRODUCTION   1

1   IMPACT OF INCARCERATION ON HEALTH   7
Inmate Health, 7
The Legal Basis for Healthcare for Inmates, 9
Continuity of Care, 10
Quality of Correctional Healthcare, 12
Healthcare Providers, 13

2   VULNERABLE POPULATIONS AND OPPORTUNITIES FOR REDUCING HEALTH RISKS   15
Mental Illness and Addiction, 16
Older Adults, 21
Women, 23
Youth, 25
Families, 25
Release and Re-Entry, 26
Cultures of Care, 28

3   ACCESS TO HEALTHCARE   31
Medicaid Enrollment, 31
Workforce, 33
Quality of Care and Accountability, 34
States and Health Plans, 35

Cost Shifts, Savings, and Recidivism, 35
Equity and Rights, 36

CLOSING   37

BIBLIOGRAPHY   41

APPENDIX: Workshop Agenda and Participants   49

Introduction

Incarceration rates in the United States are remarkably high. Those incarcerated present an array of poor health conditions, including mental illness, addiction, and chronic disease. While incarcerated, they can face additional health challenges. Unfortunately, there is a dearth of knowledge about the quantity, quality, or outcomes of healthcare within correctional systems. The situation of prisoners has a public health impact on their families and communities, both while they are incarcerated and after their release. Upon release, these individuals' health needs continue, although their access to care can be interrupted or limited. A changing policy environment, particularly the pending implementation of the Patient Protection and Affordable Care Act (ACA), creates an opportunity to improve outcomes both for public safety and for public health.

A half-day workshop was held on December 5, 2012, to address the challenges and opportunities for improving health and healthcare of the incarcerated. Sixteen invited presenters spoke in a roundtable fashion (see Appendix for workshop agenda and participants). An additional 25 people attended the workshop to observe the discussion. Participants included academics, practitioners, state officials, and nongovernmental organization representatives from the fields of healthcare, prisoner advocacy, and corrections. This report summarizes the presentations and discussion during the workshop. It also refers to the background paper distributed prior to the workshop, "Incarceration and Health," by Josiah Rich, Dora Dumont, and Scott Allen, as well as to participants' slide presentations shared at the workshop (Rich, Dumont, and Allen, 2012).

One purpose of the workshop was to inform a consensus committee pulled together by the National Research Council (NRC), which is now examining the causes and consequences of high rates of incarceration in the United States. The charge given to that study committee is provided in Box I-1 and covers a broad range of consequences, including those on the health, both physical and mental, of incarcerated populations. The committee will produce its own report at the conclusion of its study. The committee asked workshop presenters to review what is known about the health of incarcerated individuals, the healthcare they receive, and effects

---

BOX I-1
Committee on Causes and Consequences of
High Rates of Incarceration
Statement of Task

An *ad hoc* panel will conduct a study and prepare a report that will focus on the scientific evidence that exists on the use of incarceration in the United States and will propose a research agenda on the use of incarceration and alternatives to incarceration for the future. The study will explore the causes of the dramatic increases in incarceration rates since the 1970s, the costs and benefits of the nation's current sentencing and incarceration policies, and whether there is evidence that alternative policies would more effectively promote public safety and community wellbeing.

Recognizing that research evidence will vary in its strength and consistency, the panel will undertake the following tasks:

1. Describe and assess the existing research on the causes, drivers, and social context of incarceration in the United States over the past 30-40 years. To what extent does existing research suggest that incarceration rates were influenced by historical and contemporary changes in:
   a. operations of criminal justice system and other public sector systems that may affect rates of arrest or conviction, and nature and severity of sanctions: such as patterns of policing, prosecution, sentencing, prison operations, and parole practices;
   b. legal and judicial policies: such as changes in law, institutional policies and practices, and judicial rulings affecting conditions for arrest, sanctions for various crimes, drug enforcement policies, and policies regarding parole and parole revocation; and
   c. social and economic structure and political conditions: such as criminal behavior, cultural shifts, changes in political attitudes and behavior, changes in public opinion, demographic changes, and changes in the structure of economic opportunity.

of incarceration on public health; and based on that evidence to identify opportunities to improve healthcare for these populations.

This report has been prepared by the workshop rapporteur as a factual summary of what occurred at the workshop. The planning committee's role was limited to planning and convening the workshop. The views contained in the report are those of individual workshop participants and do not necessarily represent the views of all workshop participants, the planning committee, or the NRC and IOM.

The committee's study and the workshop have taken place during a period of unprecedented increase in the levels of imprisonment within

---

2. Describe and assess the existing research on the consequences of current U.S. incarceration policies. To what extent does the research suggest that incarceration rates have effects on:
    a. crime rates: such as to what extent this is due to deterrence and incapacitation, to rehabilitation, or to criminogenic effects of incarceration;
    b. individual behavior and outcomes, during imprisonment and afterward: such as changes in mental and physical health, prospects for future employment, civic participation, and desistance/reoffending;
    c. families: such as effects on intimate partners and children, patterns of marriage and dating, and intergenerational effects;
    d. communities: such as geographic concentrations, neighborhood effects, effects on specific racial and ethnic communities, high rates of re-entry and return in some communities, labor markets, and patterns of crime and policing; and
    e. society: such as (in addition to effects on the crime rate) the financial and economic costs of incarceration, effects on U.S. civic life and governance, and other near-term and longer-term social costs and benefits.
3. Explore the public policy implications of the analysis of causes and consequences, including evidence for the effectiveness and costs of alternative policies affecting incarceration rates. What does the research tell us about:
    a. efficacy of policies that may affect incarceration or serve as alternatives to incarceration, including their effects on public safety and their other social benefits and costs;
    b. cost-effectiveness of specific programmatic approaches to reducing the rate of incarceration;
    c. how best to measure and assess the potential costs and benefits of alternative policies and programs; and
    d. ways to improve oversight and administration of policies, institutions, and programs affecting the rate of incarceration.

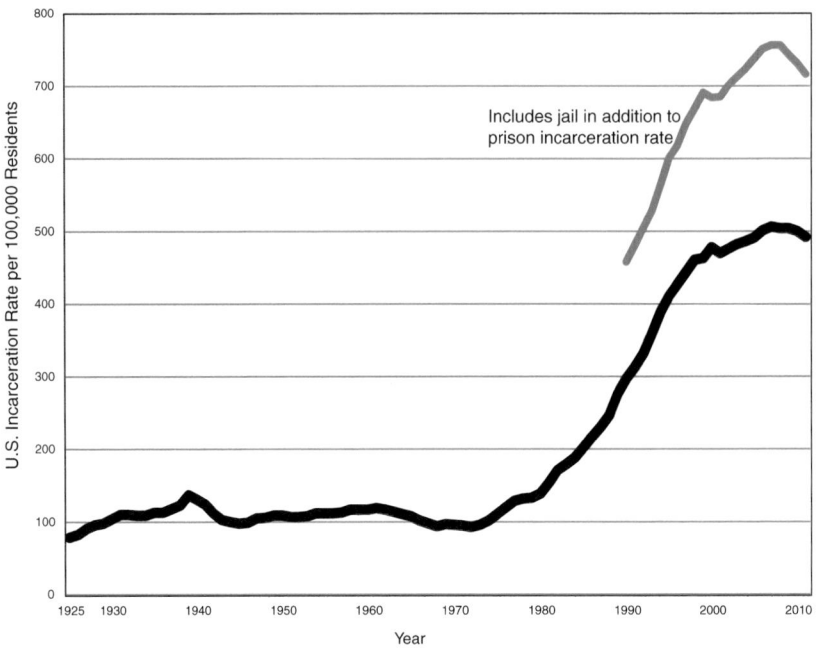

FIGURE I-1 Growth in U.S. incarceration rate.
SOURCE: Created from data in Maguire (2011).

the United States. Any accounting of the numbers involved in the U.S. correctional system shows the remarkable and historically high rates of incarceration in the United States (see, for example, Figure I-1). The Bureau of Justice Statistics reports that nearly 7 million individuals were under the supervision of the U.S. adult correctional system at year-end in 2011. This total figure includes 2.2 million inmates, with 1.5 million in prison and 700,000 in jail. Of the remaining 4.8 million, 4 million were on probation and 800,000 on parole (Carson and Sabol, 2012). Although the number of individuals in jail at any point in time is much lower than the number in prison, a great many more people flow through jails (James, 2004). For example, the Bureau of Justice Statistics reports that in the 12 months from June 2010 to June 2011, the average daily confined inmate population in county and city jails was about 735,000. However all admissions reported for that same period totaled 11.8 million, or about 16 times the size of the daily jail inmate population (Minton, 2012).

The authors of the workshop background paper argue that the failure of the U.S. healthcare system to adequately treat mental illness and addiction contributed to the escalation of the incarceration rate (Rich, Dumont, and Allen, 2012). Closing of mental hospitals in the 1970s (deinstitutionalization) was intended to shift patients to more humane care in the community; however, the authors argue that insufficient funding left many people without access to treatment. They note that individuals with mental health problems may engage in behaviors that draw attention and police responses and assert that many health professionals now feel such behavioral disorders have become criminalized.

The background paper provides evidence that many of those incarcerated have substance dependence as defined by the Diagnostic and Statistical Manual (Rich, Dumont, and Allen, 2012). Despite a body of evidence demonstrating that addiction is a chronic brain disease that can be effectively treated, the authors argue, substance dependence is often viewed as a moral failing rather than a medical issue. They believe this perception contributes to the low availability of treatment in the community. As a result, they assert drug dependence remains largely in the hands of the criminal justice system rather than the healthcare system and is criminalized rather than medicalized.

Jails provide unique challenges and opportunities for health. The stays are often too short to provide much screening or treatment; however, the very large numbers of people passing through jails with a tremendous burden of disease provide opportunities to have a significant public health impact. Healthcare opportunities and challenges for vulnerable populations who enter jails or have contact with other parts of the criminal justice system were discussed throughout the workshop.

This workshop summary has three chapters. Chapter 1 provides a brief overview of prisoner health, including the impact of incarceration on health. It then considers healthcare, including the legal basis for its provision, some aspects of its availability during incarceration, and the dilemmas experienced by many healthcare practitioners as they seek to provide quality care within correctional facilities. Chapter 2 considers a variety of proposals and models for improving the health and healthcare of vulnerable populations affected by incarceration, with particular attention to workforce issues and the importance of the continuity of care. And finally, Chapter 3 is devoted to the ACA, which received considerable attention in the workshop for its perceived potential to significantly improve inmates' access to healthcare, support changes in the workforce, reach inmates' families and communities, and possibly lead to a shift in inmates' right to care.

1

Impact of Incarceration on Health

As reported by several participants, individuals enter correctional facilities with many health problems; and incarceration has an impact on their health. Evidence was presented that many are released (especially from jails, given the high turnover rate)—and too often are re-incarcerated—with pressing health needs. Participants in the workshop discussed the impact of incarceration on inmate health and the healthcare they receive. Attention was given to possible improvement as well as deterioration in inmates' health, the legal basis for such care, the provision of it, and the context for delivering healthcare. In particular, the discussion explored the dilemmas that arise in trying to improve health within correctional institutions and the responsibility of healthcare providers to engage in improving the healthcare of incarcerated populations and the health of the communities they come from.

INMATE HEALTH

As observed in the background paper, in the absence of systematic review, perhaps it can simply be said that overall physical health probably improves during incarceration in some ways but deteriorates in others. For people living especially chaotic lives, incarceration can provide a respite and stabilization: available meals, a structured day, and reduced access to alcohol, drugs, and cigarettes, in addition to access to healthcare, especially for black men who on average have lower access than white men outside of prison (Rich, Dumont, and Allen, 2012).

Christopher Wildeman (Yale University) suggested that correctional facilities may present "a unique opportunity" to provide these individuals with "at least some medical care that they haven't gotten otherwise." Indeed, as Bruce Western (Harvard University) observed in his introductory remarks, "Prisons are coming to function as a massive organ of delivery for public health for people who are involved in the criminal justice system." Newton Kendig (Federal Bureau of Prisons) outlined the public health opportunities for both jails and prisons. He noted that jails provide a strategic public health opportunity to screen and diagnose infectious diseases among persons who often evade traditional healthcare systems and yet are at high risk for illnesses, such as HIV infection and viral hepatitis, and prisons provide an opportunity to diagnose and treat chronic diseases, such as diabetes, hypertension, addiction, and mental illness among persons who frequently have not sought or had access to treatment prior to incarceration. The structured life of prison provides an opportunity for better compliance with taking prescribed medications and eating a healthy diet as well as engagement in drug treatment services, frequent recreation, and increasingly a tobacco-free environment.

On the other hand, the prison environment may have adverse effects on health as discussed in the background paper (Rich, Dumont, Allen, 2012). The nutritional value of meals is far from ideal, because energy-dense (high-fat, high-calorie) foods are still common in prison meals. Smoking also remains a serious problem, despite the trend toward smoke-free correctional facilities. Poor ventilation, overcrowding, and stress may exacerbate chronic health conditions. More evidence is available regarding the effects of incarceration on mental health. Two conditions are especially associated with a serious degeneration of mental health: overcrowding and isolation units. The association between crowding and suicide or psychiatric commitment has been noted at least since the 1980s. Strains on staffing and facilities have particularly serious repercussions on wait times and holding conditions for the mentally ill. Case studies have also revealed widespread and serious reactions to segregation units, in which inmates are restricted to isolation cells for 23 hours a day. The restriction of movement and deprivation of human contact triggers psychological responses, ranging from anxiety and panic to hallucination. A review of health effects of incarceration also must consider sexual assault and intentional injury, either self-inflicted or resulting from assault.

Prison health conditions and impacts were further discussed at the workshop. Jamie Fellner (Human Rights Watch) described prisons as "toxic environments" with a negative impact on inmate health. She underscored the damage that can result from isolated confinement: "We know that [solitary confinement] is bad for people who are mentally ill and can cause adverse symptoms for those who didn't have prior symptoms of mental illness." Fellner also shared research findings on other aspects of prison experience, including violence (noting that one in ten state prisoners is injured in a fight) and sexual abuse (about 9.6 percent of former prisoners self-report that they were sexually abused by staff or inmates [Bureau of Justice Statistics, 2012]; those abuses were frequently accompanied by physical injuries in addition to any injury that came from penetration itself). Excessive use of force by staff is also a problem, she noted, from "old-fashioned beating" to the use of tasers and pepper sprays that can cause serious injury, particularly depending on inmates' physical conditions. "Obviously brutality has declined markedly in U.S. prisons in the last 20 years," Fellner observed, "but it still exists and it still has health consequences." Fellner also reviewed a range of other conditions in prisons that can be detrimental to inmate physical and mental health, including poor diets, poor sanitation, infestations with bugs and vermin, poor ventilation, tension, noise, lack of privacy, lack of family visits, and cross-gender pat searches (traumatizing especially for the high percentage of women in prison who have been previously sexually abused). Fellner offered these as "just some of the examples of the kinds of conditions, some caused by inattention and poor management by prison staff, and some caused by prison policies" that can be harmful to inmate health.

THE LEGAL BASIS FOR HEALTHCARE FOR INMATES

In prisons and jails, according to Robert Greifinger (John Jay College of Criminal Justice, City University of New York), "we have a litigation-driven healthcare system." Craig Haney (University of California, Santa Cruz) echoed this view, noting that "for better or worse, a lot of the access that I have into prisons has come in the context of litigation. I get called in to look at prison systems, what's happening to people in them, how those systems are functioning when—in at least someone's opinion—they're not functioning very well."

The 1976 Supreme Court decision in *Estelle v. Gamble* found that deliberate indifference to serious medical needs constitutes a violation of the Eighth Amendment prohibition of cruel and unusual punishment. *Estelle v. Gamble* led to expanded healthcare services, especially through a series of subsequent lawsuits or threatened litigation. The duty of correctional facilities to provide healthcare was recently reinforced in *Brown v. Plata* (2011), which ordered California to reduce overcrowding in prisons because of the associated failure to provide adequate healthcare to all inmates.

Acknowledging that litigation under the U.S. Constitution has driven much of the provision of healthcare services in prisons, Fellner nonetheless asserted that "the U.S. constitutional floor is so low that it is not one to which the medical profession should limit itself, and nor should government officials limit themselves to that." She cited elements from a number of international human rights treaties and guidelines addressing prisoners.[1] They call for prisoners to be treated with dignity and respect for their humanity; "Starting and ending there would be a huge step forward in many prisons, I'm afraid," she said. International treaties forbid torture or cruel, inhuman, or degrading treatment of prisoners. They also affirm that rehabilitation must be the paramount goal of incarceration and that prisoners have a right to healthcare that is accessible, available, and meets community standards. Feller noted that such standards are not strictly enforceable by U.S. judges. In some instances, the United States has signed but not ratified treaties. The elements of these international treaties are nonetheless available, and Feller urged workshop participants to heed them when generating implications for program and policy.

While the Supreme Court decision directs healthcare provision for incarcerated populations in both prisons and jails, it does not extend to those under supervision (on parole, probation, or home confinement) within the criminal justice system. As Faye Taxman (George Mason University) underscored, "People in community corrections are the largest population in the justice system, and they don't have the constitutional mandate for care that people who are incarcerated have."

CONTINUITY OF CARE

Some correctional facilities are important public health collaborators in the screening and diagnosis of infectious and other diseases, and many correctional healthcare providers across the country are highly trained and deeply committed to their patients' wellbeing. Some correctional facilities have sought partnerships with community-based medical and public health practitioners to ensure that care begun during incarceration is continued following release. Overall, however, as discussed and documented in the background paper, a disconnect exists between correctional healthcare and state or local public health departments in planning and delivering care to inmates while incarcerated and upon release (Rich, Dumont, and Allen, 2012). In particular:

---

[1] These treaties include the International Covenant on Civil and Political Rights (ICCPR), the Convention Against Torture and Other Cruel, Inhuman or Degrading Treatment or Punishment (CAT), the International Covenant on Economic and Social Rights (ICESR), and the Convention on the Rights of People with Disabilities.

- Testing policies and procedures remain inconsistent across states and facilities. Even wide-scale screening does not ensure that appropriate treatment is being provided once conditions have been diagnosed. In jails, where many people remain for under 48 hours, testing follow-through (delivery of results and establishment of a treatment regime) is especially challenging.
- Limited resources and resultant understaffing appear widespread across correctional facilities. However, there is a lack of data and appropriate measures sufficient to determine the extent of shortcomings in correctional healthcare. Health outcomes associated with staffing shortages were highlighted in testimony in *Brown v. Plata*, which specifically linked overcrowding and insufficient healthcare provider staffing. *Brown v. Plata* further noted that the conditions of care created by overcrowding had created a staff culture of "cynicism and fear," which made it even more difficult to attract competent clinicians, and presumably affected the care provided by existing staff.
- Treatment for substance dependence is consistently insufficient to meet prisoner need. Despite a body of evidence demonstrating that addiction is a chronic brain disease that can be effectively treated, surveys have found that few correctional facilities have adopted evidence-based treatments, relying more frequently upon less-effective drug education services (Chandler, Fletcher, and Volkow, 2009; McCarty and Chandler, 2009). Moreover, detoxification and symptoms of withdrawal are most often treated with analgesics. This does not address the underlying addiction and leaves prisoners vulnerable to relapse and overdose upon release.

As workshop participants discussed healthcare provided in different settings and to different populations, transitions were a recurring shared concern. Haney declared transitions to be "the weakest points," as "the very best intentions flounder at the point at which there is a pass off." Haney noted this weakness at every stage: when the inmate enters the system, then "when somebody moves from one facility to another, or even within a facility to another part of the institution, and certainly when somebody moves from the general [prison] population to a segregated housing unit." Release is a further highly vulnerable transition. In Haney's assessment, "No matter how good the care was, no matter how much information and intelligence was gathered about the patient, even in [well] functioning systems, there is a tremendous falloff in terms of the quality of care" at transition points. As "sometimes those transitional moments are the moments of greatest vulnerability," Haney asserted "that drop-off in care occurs at exactly the moment at which the patient needs the most care or the most attention."

QUALITY OF CORRECTIONAL HEALTHCARE

A recurrent and sustained theme throughout the workshop concerned the dilemma inherent in providing healthcare within environments that may in many ways undermine inmate health.

Haney offered a blunt statement of "the elephant in the room: prisons are not just hospitals with electrified fences around them." As he elaborated, correctional facilities are for the most part characterized by a culture that tends to create limited communication and collaboration between healthcare providers and the custody staff who operate the facility. In this setting, healthcare providers have less authority, unlike in any other setting in which they are accustomed to practicing. This affects both their ability to do their job and patients' confidence in healthcare providers. And that, observed Haney, "cycles back oftentimes even in the best trained and most well-intentioned care providers to a change in attitude about the patient." However, it should be noted that the healthcare providers at the workshop welcomed the incarcerated population as patients in need of care.

Furthermore, in Haney's view, some prison environments "are so inhospitable that it is impossible to deliver effective medical and mental health care." Citing particularly the "two extremes of confinement: hopelessly overcrowded prison systems and conditions of long-term segregation or isolation," Haney argued that the norms, policies, culture, and even architecture of prisons can worsen health problems among the ill, and even generate problems among the healthy. Thus, it simply "becomes impossible to effectively deliver treatment in those kinds of environments."

Fellner offered a similar account of the environment and culture within correctional facilities, and the resulting dilemma for doctors. In her view, "prisons are ill-equipped by virtue of [a broad] mission, their culture, their training, their reward systems, their bureaucracies" to undertake the delivery of healthcare services to all prisoners who need them. Therefore, while correctional facilities aim to provide adequate healthcare and may even recognize their interests are served by having a healthier inmate population, other purposes, environments complicated by the rise in incarceration rates, and limited resources compromise reaching that end.

HEALTHCARE PROVIDERS

The workshop discussion sharpened to focus on providers' professional and ethical responsibilities to advance the quality of correctional healthcare. Greifinger added two factors to the difficulty of providing healthcare effectively within correctional facilities. One is the lack of leadership, as "the commissioners, secretaries, and wardens often are not providing the leadership to allow the modern innovative value-driven physicians and other healthcare practitioners to do their jobs." Another is the pronounced isolation of healthcare providers in prison and jail settings, as they are often separated from their peers practicing in the general public.

Above all, however, Greifinger underscored the adverse effects of the culture of correctional facilities, particularly the "stereotyping and cynicism that results in distrust." As Greifinger reflected, "I've been involved in a lot of litigation over the years, class-action suits and individual cases. I can tell you that in the individual cases, 99 percent of the time the reasons there was unconstitutional care was because there was mistrust and cynicism of what the patient was saying. So I think we have a real danger of a lot of harm continuing unless we change the system of care."

Scott Allen (University of California, Riverside) directly addressed the medical profession's responsibility in establishing the current system. Declaring that the system was created "on our watch," Allen explained that historically doctors were involved in the initiation of both prisons and asylums, and that "doctors remain essential, and even we would argue foundational, to the continued existence of jails and prisons." Allen described the crux of the dilemma as the effort to provide care with and within institutions with practices that can be more punitive rather than therapeutic. As the system became established, "the medical profession went along for the ride." Indeed, declared Allen, "I see this as a failure of the medical profession as a whole."

Specifically, Allen reviewed four aspects of medical professionalism and how they are tested by the prison system: (1) altruism and commitment to patient interest; (2) physician self-regulation; (3) maintenance of technical competence; and (4) civic engagement. In Allen's view, within correctional institutions, "altruism and loyalty to the patient's interest is fine as long as they don't come into conflict with the institutional mission." There is some support for physicians' self-regulation, and a good deal of emphasis on technical competence. Civic engagement, however, is "the first to go," as doctors providing healthcare within correctional facilities are "often reminded whether directly or indirectly to stay in our lane, that we're not there to make policy suggestions, just treat the patients, just take care of them." In Allen's view, to accept that constriction of civil engagement is to forgo both the moral authority and the legal authority of the medical profession within the criminal justice system. To Allen's dismay, "I don't think historically we have leveraged that or asserted that [authority]."

Haney puzzled over this situation, calling for "help figuring out how to operate effectively" in such adverse environments. Fellner agreed, noting that this is "something which medical professionals have to work on." She articulated a challenge to healthcare providers: "You're no longer guests in the house of corrections, you have as much right to be there as the guards, you're constitutionally required, and it means speaking up more." Healthcare professionals working within correctional facilities and those observing the situation from the outside have, in her view, "an obligation to inform themselves and speak out" on conditions of confinement and impediments to appropriate healthcare delivery.

Speaking from the vantage point of a medical professional seeking to provide healthcare within correctional facilities, Allen affirmed "it's important we take ownership of our role. We went along for the ride, we were always integrated as a profession, and we need to take ownership and acknowledge that." The next step is to "assert our medical leadership," including exercising both moral and legal authority. Noting the medical profession's past "failure to civically engage on both the policy and political level," Allen called for doctors to become engaged "in greater number, with greater emphasis, and greater authority, so that we move forward and promote policies that are in the interest of our patients." Such policies, Allen asserted, will address not only conditions of confinement and delivery of healthcare within correctional facilities, but also transition of care for those released back to the community, and above all, "all the things that lead to the risk of incarceration in the first place."

2

Vulnerable Populations and Opportunities for Reducing Health Risks

Workshop participants identified many immediate opportunities and models for addressing health needs of those involved in the criminal justice system. Proposals addressed care and health interventions for a range of vulnerable populations, including not only inmates but also their families as well as those recently released. Many of these proposals involved changes to the workforce, such as retraining parole officers, educating judges, raising the skill of screeners, and hiring former inmates as community health workers. Throughout the discussion, workshop participants expressed awareness of the potential of many measures to perform a threefold function: prevent incarceration in the first place; treat the health needs of the currently incarcerated, their families, and the released; and prevent recidivism.

As a preliminary note, Newton Kendig reminded participants of the great range of inmates: "Incarcerated populations are extremely diverse, depending on geography, ethnicity, gender, and healthcare needs." Correctional facilities are also very varied, from prisons holding inmates serving lengthy sentences to local jails with their "hyperdynamic population movement." Finally, regional variations are also significant. For example, "in Appalachia, methamphetamine oral healthcare could be the number one issue at intake. In an inner city area, it could be HIV and Hepatitis C. On the border of Mexico it's drug-resistant TB." Thus, Kendig warned, it is likely not all proposals or priorities will apply across the correctional system.

The health needs of inmates with a history of mental illness or addiction received considerable attention in the workshop, as did the health profile of older adults, women, and youth in prisons and jails, and families of those incarcerated, as well as individuals recently released from prisons or jails.

MENTAL ILLNESS AND ADDICTION

Overrepresentation

The overrepresentation of people with behavioral disorders in the correction systems was the focus of a workshop presentation by Fred Osher (Council of State Governments' Justice Center). Osher explained that 5 percent of the general population are estimated to have a serious mental illness (Kessler et al., 1996); and while the rates are not directly comparable, other studies have shown that the rate is much higher among the incarcerated population, and especially so among women. In state prisons, 24 percent of women and 16 percent of men have a serious mental illness (Ditton, 1999). In jails, 31 percent of women and 15 percent of men have a serious mental illness (Steadman et al., 2009). Osher noted, "We don't understand that exactly, but we've clearly got a big challenge with this gender disparity and responding in appropriate ways to the needs of women in correctional settings."

Osher also offered estimates for substance abuse among prisoners, observing that while less than 20 percent of the general population suffer addiction, the figure in prisons and jails approaches 50 percent (Karberg and James, 2005; Mumola and Karberg, 2006). Co-occurring mental disorder and substance abuse is also very high. In the general population, about 25 percent of those with a serious mental illness have a co-occurring disorder, while in jails, more than 70 percent of those with a serious mental illness have a co-occurring disorder (Kessler et al., 1996; Ditton, 1999; James and Glaze, 2006; Steadman et al., 2009). Again, the rates are not directly comparable across different studies and time periods, but the potential differences are striking. The co-occurrence of mental disorder and substance abuse can complicate the detection of either, particularly when staff or diagnostic instruments are insufficiently sensitive, or where overcrowding and/or understaffing reduces the time spent on medical screening. Osher termed such co-occurrence a "critical issue" that needs to be addressed at points of both entry and exit from the correctional system.

While Osher's figures highlighted those with serious mental illness (e.g., major affective disorders or schizophrenia), Fellner broadened attention to inmates whose mental health problems are less severe but might still lead to significant functional disabilities. This describes over half the incarcerated population. Fellner provided figures indicating that 56 percent of state prisoners have a mental health problem. Again, rates are substantially higher among women inmates, as 73 percent of women and 55 percent of men in state prisons have mental health problems (James and Glaze, 2006).

The overrepresentation of the mentally ill among the incarcerated is a prominent trend across the country though rates of mental illness vary somewhat across state and federal prisons and local jails. As Shannon Murphy (Montgomery County's Prerelease and Reentry Center, Rockville, Maryland) observed, in the relative paucity of either mental health facilities or community support systems, prisons are now "the de facto chronic mental health system" in the United States. Craig Haney further suggested that the magnitude of the problem is undercounted and underestimated. In Haney's view, the underestimate "creates a kind of ripple effect through the problem. If resources aren't adequate to the task at hand then there is a way in which that unsolved problem tends to get greater rather than simply stay in its underestimated size." Haney cited as an example the "so-called California overcrowding case" that culminated at the Supreme Court (*Brown v. Plata*), but which actually began as a mental health case. Litigation to ensure constitutionally adequate care for mentally ill prisoners brought attention to runaway overcrowding that exacerbated mental health and medical problems and caused the level of care to fall below constitutional standards.

Reflecting on the disproportionate numbers of people with untreated or undertreated mental health problems and addiction in the prison population, Allen noted that, given the lack of adequate care, "what we're left with is a very large number of people with compelling health needs who are ultimately incarcerated in institutions whose mission is security and where [medical] treatment is an afterthought if it even occurs at all." This theme of an inherent tension of attempting to provide therapeutic care within institutions organized for security recurred throughout the workshop (see further discussion below).

Treatment

Redonna Chandler (National Institute on Drug Abuse, National Institutes of Health) framed the value of addressing mental illness and addiction succinctly: "What are the health issues that if we addressed them could help to deal with some of the root causes of incarceration? Addiction and mental health are two of the primary health conditions. If those can be effectively addressed within the community, then you can lower the number of people who are incarcerated and the number of people who are re-incarcerated because of violating conditions of supervised release."

Participants offered several proposals to address mental illness and addiction before, during, and after incarceration.

Osher offered a somewhat different perspective: "What I want to say as a main point here is that it's just not as simple as we'd like it to be. Just treating mental illness or substance abuse disorders may not in and of itself be our solution to [reducing the prevalence of individuals with behavioral disorders in the criminal justice system]." Osher grounded this view in results of a study of inmates in Hawaii with schizophrenia spectrum disorder. The study suggested that for two-thirds of these inmates, factors other than mental illness or substance abuse had led to their initial incarceration or recidivism. Those factors, Osher emphasized, are the very same factors that explain why people without behavioral disorders become incarcerated. Osher identified these as the "central eight dynamic risk factors" that account for much of the variance in people becoming incarcerated: antisocial attitudes, antisocial friends and peers, antisocial personality patterns, substance abuse, family and marital factors, lack of education, poor employment history, and lack of pro-social leisure activities. Each of these risk factors, Osher emphasized, can be addressed through interventions. Osher further acknowledged that people with mental illness tend to have significantly more of the central eight dynamic risk factors.

To address these dynamic risk factors, Osher proposed adherence to the principles of the Risk-Needs-Responsivity Model (Andrews, 2006; Andrews and Bonta, 2006). The Risk Principle consists of screening an individual inmate's risk of reoffending and matching the intervention to that level of risk. The Needs Principle consists of targeting the inmate's criminogenic needs. According to Osher, the more criminogenic needs are targeted, the larger the effect of the intervention. The Responsivity Principle calls for tailoring the intervention to the learning style, motivation, culture, demographic, and abilities of the individual inmate. Osher clarified that while mental illness itself is not a criminogenic risk, and not one of the central eight dynamic risk factors, it can have a major impact on responsivity. Thus, "mental illness must be addressed so that the individual can fully engage in the interventions that are associated with reduced recidivism."

Osher offered further advice on applying the Risk-Needs-Responsivity Model, particularly because of the potential to actually increase the rate of recidivism. According to Osher, "we know in fact that if you don't attend to risk that you can actually do harm. We know that the largest impact on recidivism takes place when the focus is those individuals with [higher risk levels] and that one can actually increase recidivism if low risk individuals are the focus of treatment." Osher referred to results from a study in Ohio to support this view (Latessa, 2012). He concluded that "we should prioritize and use scarce resources most effectively to get the public health and public safety outcomes that we want." That will involve developing the skillsets of those involved in providing the interventions, particularly interventions based in cognitive behavioral therapy. In Osher's view, "there's a large workforce development issue that we need to be mindful of."

During discussion, Taxman highlighted the varying definitions of and perspectives on the concept of an antisocial personality, as well as the "diverse and inconsistent measurement of that particular domain." Taxman also observed that it is a "very controversial issue in the field, whether or not mental illness is a criminogenic need or not, whether or not treating mental illness will reduce recidivism rates." Her sense is that "over the last ten years I think the field has moved in a direction recognizing that [mental illness and criminogenic risk] are different entities."

Taxman concurred with Osher regarding the imperative of developing the workforce to provide effective behavioral interventions. She particularly discussed retraining probation officers and parole officers to undertake roles as social workers and behavioral managers, rather than perform as agents of enforcement and security. "When probation officers and parole officers use behavioral management techniques," Taxman declared, "it works." In accordance with the Risk-Needs-Responsivity Model, Taxman suggested that correctional staff should identify the risks and needs of individuals, and then work with them to develop "problem-solving techniques." An essential component of the process is instilling a sense of responsibility in the individual. According to Taxman, if the individual is to be compliant "for everything from [not] offending through [following through with] primary healthcare, then really the individual needs to have much more responsibility." She therefore advocated less of a focus on any particular program for inmates, and greater effort to have probation and parole officers "help people make choices in their lives, how they are going to get through probation successfully." Taxman saw great potential when supervising officers are trained less as agents of social control, and more as facilitators of behavioral change with an emphasis on helping individuals exercise responsibility and self-determination. According to Taxman, "If we don't change the criminal justice policies . . . that focus just on monitoring conditions of release, then we're not going to make progress toward a system so that people can take care of their own needs outside of the criminal justice system." If this could be accomplished, Taxman argued, inmates could "find a way to become more contributing members of society and find value in their own lives." Currently, however, "that's not something the criminal justice system is invested in doing."

Addressing substance abuse effectively was another priority

addressed in the workshop. Participants noted that there are many evidence-based treatments for substance abuse, both behavioral treatments and medication-assisted treatments. As Chandler lamented, however, "the capacity for delivering those treatments is limited and fragmented." The delivery of evidence-based behavioral treatments is poor; the delivery of medication-assisted treatments is even worse. This is the case even though, explained Chandler, "we know that medication can help address opiate addiction, alcohol, as well as nicotine. It's one of the most effective interventions we have. Yet when you look at the number of individuals that could potentially benefit, only a very small portion is being served." Thus, expanding substance abuse treatment, including medication-assisted treatment, is critical.

Chandler dwelt further on the imperative of providing continuing treatment during re-entry. As she explained, "Study after study after study has shown that if you only provide treatment to an individual while they're incarcerated and you don't follow that up with ongoing care when they re-enter the community, you are not going to be able to significantly impact their drug use." Two factors are closely linked to relapse. One is the cue-rich environments to which addicts return, cues that the underlying neurobiological mechanisms in their brains have associated with their drug use, triggering craving. The second is the incredibly stressful situation of re-entry itself, which also triggers neurobiological responses that lead to an increased risk of relapse.

Workforce issues also figured in the discussion of substance abuse treatment. "It's really important," Chandler affirmed, "to make sure that criminal justice actors, and especially leaders, understand the underlying and important health problems of this population." Unfortunately, addiction is widely misunderstood. In her assessment, "very few people outside of the healthcare field—and even within the healthcare field—understand the underlying neurobiological principles of addictive disorders. If they don't understand that they see it as moral failing, they blame the individual, and then they're reticent to provide treatment or to be open to other types of models of care." Because of her years of involvement in training judges, Chandler appreciates the value of such training. She described, "seeing the light bulb go off in their heads," and their subsequent return to their jurisdictions to enact "radical changes in the way they deal with the problem of drug abuse because they understand the underlying biological processes that are occurring." Chandler concluded, "Where there is ignorance I think we have the opportunity to shed some light, and that's going to be really important if you want these partnerships and collaborations, and if you really want to be able to optimize outcomes."

OLDER ADULTS

The proportion of older adults in the criminal justice system, and resultant healthcare concerns, have increased sharply (see Figure 2-1). In her presentation, Brie Williams (University of California, San Francisco) described the trend. From 1990 to 2012, the U.S. population age 55 or older increased by about 50 percent. In that same period, the U.S. prisoner population age 55 or older in the state and federal prison systems increased by some 550 percent as the prison population doubled. "This increasing number of older adults," Williams declared, "really changes the entire health landscape of the correctional system."

Williams explored several characteristics of the disease burden of older adult inmates. First, as in the general population, older inmates have the highest rates of typical chronic health conditions (congestive heart failure, diabetes, chronic obstructive pulmonary disease, etc.) and serious life-limiting illnesses. Second, older inmates also have very high rates of additional geriatric syndromes such as cognitive impairment or dementia, and disabilities or impaired ability to perform activities of daily living. Some of this disability is common to the general population, such

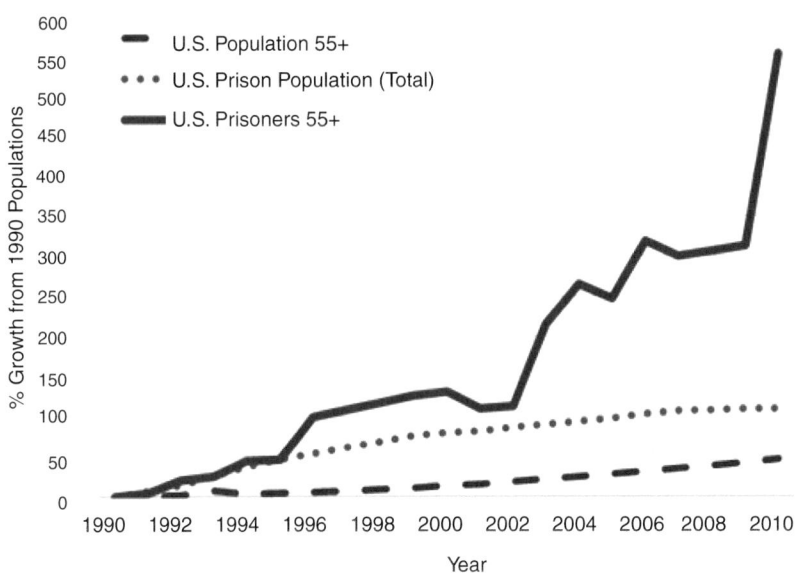

FIGURE 2-1 Rate of growth of older adults in the criminal justice system.
SOURCE: Williams et al. (2012a).

as impaired mobility or the need for assistance with eating or bathing. Other disabilities are unique to the prison environment, such as not being able to drop to the floor as instructed in response to an alarm or, worse, not being able to get back up again after the alarm is over, or difficulty climbing on or off one's assigned bunk. Because of the unique challenges of a prison environment and the resulting disabilities, Williams explained, "In older adults, simply cataloguing chronic disease is insufficient." Given aging trends of the incarcerated population and their associated health conditions, Williams observed that "correctional institutions are increasingly becoming a critical delivery site for long-term care or nursing home-level care, as well as palliative care or care for people with serious chronic illnesses."

In confronting and meeting the needs of the rapidly increasing older adult inmate population, Williams underscored the importance of examining both health and nonhealth policies of the criminal justice system. Beginning with health-related policies, Williams advocated four immediate changes. First is to screen for and address cognitive impairment and dementia, and then incorporate these screening results into court proceedings, healthcare delivery, parole, probation, and release planning. This would have extensive repercussions for workforce training, as it would involve "everyone from police and judges and attorneys, through jail and prison clinicians, and then people responsible for probation and parole."

A second imperative is to define and address disability, with attention to "what disability looks like in the correctional setting." This would involve delineating the basic physical tasks that are necessary for a person to function with independence by housing unit, and then matching these physical tasks to prisoner abilities when housing is assigned. "This seems very basic," Williams observed, "and [surprising] how infrequently it happens." A re-screening schedule should then be implemented, especially because sentences have grown longer. Very often the only disability assessment is performed at intake, even if an individual is incarcerated for decades.

Williams' third suggestion was to develop plans for long-term care and nursing home-level care, essentially a continuum of care across the spectrum of disability, with criteria for classification in different care levels. This would include enhanced palliative care or symptom-based chronic care management for people who are seriously ill. "I would love to see [the rate of incarceration decrease]," Williams remarked, "but until it does, I think we need to make these plans."

Her fourth health-related policy proposal was to create a national medical release or so-called compassionate release guideline. These uniform guidelines would be based in scientific evidence from palliative and geriatric medicine and clinical medicine in general. Barriers that prevent medically eligible persons from obtaining release would have to be addressed. Fellner concurred on the significance of compassionate release and noted that the Federal Bureau of Prisons and most states have provisions for releasing inmates in extraordinary and compelling circumstances, but that these are "greatly underutilized." Fellner urged that healthcare providers "be involved in trying to make those [provisions] work."

Williams expanded her suggestions to the nonhealth policies that have unanticipated health consequences on the growing older adult inmate population. "Good people can take different sides of each of these issues," she acknowledged. "My point is not to say which [side] of these issues is correct or not correct, but to say that these points need to be debated given the changing demographic of the population." Williams highlighted three such policies as meriting re-examination. First is sentencing decisions, as "three strikes [policies] and life without possibility of parole have really resulted in a higher concentration, very simply, of older and sicker persons across the nation in the correctional setting." Second is facility policies, such as lockdowns and administrative segregation, because "evidence suggests that these may increase disability and deconditioning specifically for older prisoners or for those with chronic impairments." Finally, a careful review of "well-meaning state-wide reorganization efforts that can be dramatic and really large in scope," but may have unintended effects—such as shifting older adult inmates from prisons to jails, "which [often] have fewer healthcare resources, especially for chronic disease management." In concluding, Williams affirmed the responsibility of the medical profession to "help with criminal justice policy, and be at the table to anticipate potential health consequences [of] both health policies [and] nonhealth policies."

WOMEN

Although female inmates are only about 10 percent of the correctional population, they present higher rates of disease and additional reproductive health issues. As noted earlier, mental health disease burden is considerably higher for women than men. Very high rates of childhood sexual abuse and post-traumatic stress disorder are prevalent among female inmates. Given the disproportionate burden of mental illness borne by women inmates, the proposals for addressing the mental health needs, discussed above, are particularly applicable to this population.

Jennifer Clarke (Brown University Medical Center) addressed health issues of incarcerated women, particularly reproductive health. Clarke estimated that 5 to 6 percent of women coming into prisons or jails are pregnant. The data on birth outcomes vary, but in general, babies weigh more the longer a woman is incarcerated. Reasons for better birth outcomes are likely better access to prenatal care, decrease in substance use, and, for some, stable housing and regular meals. Clarke hastened to note, "I always have to follow that by clarifying I am not advocating incarcerating pregnant women but rather underscoring the need for this population to have services in the community."

Clarke also commented on the research finding that most of the women who enter incarceration pregnant had conceived within three months of leaving a prior incarceration. This emphasizes the need for correctional facilities to provide family planning services, as most so-called "pregnant women days" within prisons are from women who have been imprisoned previously where a more stable diet and less access to drugs may have improved fertility, and upon release, without family planning services, conceived promptly. The stress of an unplanned pregnancy could add to their difficulty of getting re-established in the community, and some are soon re-incarcerated. Clarke shared research that indicated that about 70 percent of women in the criminal justice system who are at risk for an unplanned pregnancy indicated they want to start a contraceptive method.

Sexually transmitted infections (tested on entry to prison or jail) are about 10 to 20 times higher in the incarcerated female population than the general population, and at least twice as high as that of the incarcerated male population. As health consequences of such infections for women are much greater than they are for men, Clarke affirmed the paramount importance of screening and treating women for such infections as they enter prisons and jails.

Clarke also offered observations on the rise in obesity. Women on average gain over a pound a week when incarcerated. A year's incarceration thus results in over a 50-pound weight gain, with considerable consequences for both the physical and mental health of women inmates.

Clarke underscored the imperative of providing reproductive healthcare, with attention to continuing care after release. Recalling evidence that women expressed interest in starting a contraceptive method and also acknowledging that "there have been a lot of abuses in the past of reproductive freedom," Clarke advocated the availability of reversible contraceptive methods.

Asked about the provision of nurseries in correctional facilities, Clarke noted "great outcomes," including better bonding and more breastfeeding, when this is possible. Given the small size, limited resources, and security concerns of many facilities, however, Clarke acknowledged that nurseries are not universally feasible. She therefore concluded, "I think it's in the best interest of correctional facilities to do the preventive healthcare to prevent needing a nursery later on."

YOUTH

Youth were not a focus of presentations in the workshop. However, Chandler remarked on this lacuna, asserting "we're missing a tremendous opportunity by not talking about adolescents and juvenile justice." Taxman observed that there are more youths in the juvenile justice system than in foster care. Chandler provided figures indicating that approximately 1.5 million adolescents are involved in the juvenile justice system, either in community programs or detention centers. These youth have tremendous healthcare needs, including addiction, mental health problems, and infectious disease. If those needs are not addressed effectively, Chandler affirmed, there are two outcomes for these youth: premature violent death or involvement in the adult correctional system.

What initiatives could be undertaken to address the health needs of youths in the criminal justice system? According to Chandler, "This is the only population that we can name where we can safely say that all of the individuals in this population merit [screening for addiction and identifying] a drug abuse intervention." She advocated "comprehensive screening for all adolescents in juvenile justice to determine the severity of their substance abuse problem," to be followed by "either an indicated prevention intervention or a drug use treatment intervention." Chandler estimated that half of youth in the juvenile justice system have a substance abuse problem severe enough to warrant a diagnosis; thus, "you're going to be providing treatment to a large number of adolescents."

FAMILIES

The public health impacts of soaring incarceration rates are manifold. Relevant vulnerable populations include not only the incarcerated, but their family members as well. Christopher Wildeman (Yale University) offered several insights in his presentation on the effects of incarceration on the health of family members. Prisoners are embedded in social networks. Thus, Wildeman emphasized, for every individual inmate, a far greater number of family members may be affected. As the incarceration rate soars, so does the number of family members affected by incarceration. All of these people—the partners, children, and siblings of inmates—are drawn into the correctional system when a family member is incarcerated.

Considering the health of this population, Wildeman began by noting that they are exposed to the same risk factors for poor health as are the individuals who actually experience incarceration: the same socioeconomic status, education levels, and neighborhood exposures. This suggests a probable overlap in health problems, including mental health problems. In Wildeman's view, this is "a tremendously vulnerable population even if you assume having a family member incarcerated has no health impact on them." Increasing evidence, however, suggests that incarceration does compromise the health of family members, amplifying the public health impact of increased rate of incarceration.

Wildeman considered the potential of using the criminal justice system to find ways to improve the health of this population, even though they are not directly involved in it. He particularly proposed that the process of prisoner release might be an opportunity to gather information about family members. This could facilitate enrolling them in social services, Medicaid, or other programs. In this way, indirect contact with the criminal justice system might have some benefit for this population, particularly as the bulk of this population is not now enrolled in any healthcare plan.

RELEASE AND RE-ENTRY

As explained in the background paper, the period immediately following release from prison or jail is especially risky (Rich, Dumont, and Allen, 2012). While mortality rates within prisons and jails are comparable to those of the general population for white males and lower than their nonincarcerated peers for black males, former prisoners are nearly 13 times more likely to die in the two weeks following release than the general population (Binswanger et al., 2007). In particular, former prisoners are 129 times more likely than the general population to die of an overdose during that period. This reflects both the challenges faced upon return to communities and the insufficient nature of substance abuse treatment during incarceration, during which prisoners may not realize their tolerance to opiates has declined. Despite efforts to improve the outcomes of prisoner re-entry through assistance with employment, housing, and other transitional needs that ultimately affect health, only about 10 percent of prisoners from state prisons in need of discharge planning actually receive it (Mellow and Greifinger, 2007). In general, mentally ill prisoners and those with HIV are more likely than others to receive discharge planning. Nonetheless, they are also more likely to be homeless and rely on extensive emergency department healthcare post-release. Although inmates with mental illnesses are generally given a supply of medications upon release, medication adherence falls off rapidly upon release.

Emily Wang (Yale University) addressed the health of the newly released based on her experience and research with the Transitions Clinic Network. This is a national network of programs currently operating in six states, the District of Columbia, and Puerto Rico, based in community health centers and providing primary care to individuals post-prison. Wang confirmed that the immediate aftermath of release is a particularly risky period. She noted a worsening of chronic medical conditions and substance abuse, and a high risk of hospitalization and risk of death among the newly released. Based on her research among clients of the Transitions Clinic in San Francisco, Wang observed that many had not received any discharge planning, and had either short or no supply of medications. Among the clinic's patients, 69 percent were uninsured. For those who had been enrolled, Medicaid or Medicare Part B had lapsed while they were incarcerated. Finally, drug felons faced additional barriers to meeting their basic needs and getting access to food stamps or housing assistance. Immediately post-release, 93 percent were homeless or at risk for being homeless. Wang also discovered that 39 percent of the clinic's patients went a whole day without food.

An overriding priority in dealing with release is providing continuity of care, whatever care that might be, whether it is for treatment for addiction or mental illness, for reproductive care, or for management of chronic disease. The risks involved at the moment of re-entry, and the likelihood that healthcare would be interrupted, were reiterated several times during the workshop. Wang offered other insights from the focus groups that Transitions Clinic Network has conducted. Participants in these groups consistently express three preferences. They asked that primary care providers possess relevant cultural competence, and specifically that they have past experience caring for patients with a history of incarceration. They also requested community health workers with a history of incarceration to assist with patient navigation of the social service system and the healthcare system, as well as provide support in care management and chronic disease management. Their third request was access to primary care within the first two weeks after release.

Wang incorporated these preferences in developing suggestions for addressing the needs of inmates upon release. Her first proposal was that individuals with a past history of incarceration be involved in improving the healthcare of returning prisoners. This is an issue of workforce training and cultural competence, as well as providing former prisoners with a role in decision making or "having a seat at the table." Addressing all these issues would entail "people with experience of incarceration coupled with proper training as a community health worker to help patients navigate the healthcare system following release, and really deal with all the social issues that might emerge in those days, weeks, months post-release."

Wang's second suggestion was to improve transitions from prison to community healthcare systems. Relevant evidence-based steps start with basic discharge planning, refilling medications, and ensuring availability of medical records. Several workshop participants mentioned the possibility that electronic medical records might ease this last task. Wang also cited evidence-based methods for preparing community health centers to facilitate early access to care in the primary care setting.

As discussed more fully below in the context of the Patient Protection and Affordable Care Act, Wang's third suggestion was to eliminate barriers to Medicaid enrollment and reinstatement. Her final suggestion was to eliminate full or partial food-stamp bans and barriers to housing and employment. Even where barriers are not formal or direct, regulations—such as the requirement of specific forms of identification—can block access to food aid or other services. "Time and time again, among the patients that I'm seeing, post-release, two weeks on," Wang explained, "they've already come to the physician, they're interested in their health, and the really crippling part is there are so many other needs there that they're unable to attend to their health in the best possible way." She cited evidence of access to food, "just the barebones importance of food," as particularly crucial for this population.

Wildeman concurred, adding "if we just improve the medical care that [former inmates] receive but we don't attend to their homelessness as a passive result of incarceration, or economic instability, or labor market outcomes, or family life," then we miss much that has "a really profound effect on their health over the life course as well."

CULTURES OF CARE

A further set of suggestions emerged during workshop discussions. They dealt less with any particular inmate population, and more with how healthcare and criminal justice professionals approach the provision and context of care. Much of this involved education. For example, Williams advocated that healthcare professionals educate others about the health needs of aging inmates. She noted that as her team trains police, judges, public defenders, district attorneys, and correctional officers about dementia, "across the board people are [often] relieved to be finally getting healthcare information that [can] make their jobs both better, more rewarding, and less stressful."

In response, Wang noted that healthcare providers need to be educated about many aspects of the criminal justice system. She lamented that primary care providers practicing in federally qualified health centers are seeing patients with a past history of incarceration, perhaps recently released, and yet have no idea of the type of care these patients have received during incarceration. Wang suggested that both criminal justice professionals and healthcare providers need to develop cultural competence when dealing with this population.

Steven Rosenberg (Community Oriented Correctional Health Services) pursued the theme of cultural competence, suggesting that healthcare providers should attempt to understand not only the conditions faced by inmates while incarcerated and upon release, but also the pressures faced by criminal justice professionals—thus becoming "cross culturally competent" so as to avoid possible conflict. Allen challenged this perspective, suggesting that no change of cultural frame would eliminate the innate conflict between providing care while simultaneously fulfilling a goal of security. Such conflicts cannot be navigated past: "They're baked into the pie. There are two functions and they come into conflict."

Yet Allen agreed on the imperative of mutual respect between corrections officers and healthcare providers: "It's really important while we demand respect from custody [staff], that we're also able to return it and learn to speak their language as much as we ask them to speak ours." This is a matter of practical importance, "because you can talk all day about the ideals of medicine, but if you can't translate it into how they can actually apply what you're recommending in a way that they will still have their job at the end of the year, you're just spinning your wheels."

3

Access to Healthcare

The Patient Protection and Affordable Care Act (ACA) was recognized throughout the workshop as an unprecedented opportunity to expand health services to the population involved in the criminal justice system. Discussion was informed by both the background paper and additional papers by Regenstein and Christie-Maples (2012) and Phillips (2012). The implications of ACA were explored within the workshop, with discussion focusing on aspects of enrollment, workforce, quality of care, costs, and equity.

MEDICAID ENROLLMENT

Many prison and jail inmates are poor, lack insurance, and are in need of health services. By federal law, inmates already enrolled in Medicaid are precluded from receiving benefits while incarcerated.[1] That will not change under ACA, as currently written. As discussed in the background paper, in order to see a healthcare provider, inmates generally must submit sick call slips and often pay a fee. Such fees have been implemented in the federal system, in about 70 percent of state prisons, and an unknown number of jails. While the sums involved are usually small (e.g., $2 to $5), even this low cost has been a substantial deterrent for inmates making from 7¢ to 13¢ an hour in prison work assign-

---

[1] Note in some states, prisoners can be covered by Medicaid when they are hospitalized outside the prison.

ments (Rich, Dumont, and Allen, 2012). Some systems provide waivers for copayments, at least for some types of care such as communicable diseases and true emergency and follow-up care; copayments can also be waived for incarcerated people who are medically indigent. A 2003 Centers for Disease Control and Prevention report on a multistate outbreak of antibiotic-resistant staph infections in correctional facilities listed copays along with staff shortages as hindering access to timely care, contributing to the spread of the infection. Further, in most states, individuals entering incarceration already enrolled in Medicaid face disenrollment from the program, despite federal guidance that Medicaid coverage only be suspended, not terminated, as a result of incarceration (Phillips, 2012). With this pattern of disenrollment, almost 80 percent of those previously covered are without private or public insurance when released, exactly during the high-risk re-entry period when access to health services can be critical.

The ACA presents a major opportunity for millions of poor people to obtain insurance coverage. When fully enacted in 2014, ACA will raise Medicaid eligibility levels to 133 percent of the poverty line for all adults. States will receive a 100 percent federal subsidy to cover the expansion of Medicaid enrollment for the first three years and a tapering subsidy thereafter. A substantial percentage of those newly eligible for Medicaid will have some involvement with prisons or jails. The potential of the ACA to reach these individuals is great but also has limits. Some of these limits are formal, including legal restrictions on accessing benefits. Other possible barriers may include limits to the ability to facilitate the Medicaid enrollment process within correctional facilities.

As delineated in the paper by Regenstein and Christie-Maples (2012), jail inmates who are held pending disposition (estimated at from one-half to two-thirds of the jail population) may face formal restrictions to accessing benefits. The authors make the following distinctions among inmates pending disposition:

- Incarcerated individuals pending disposition are qualified to enroll in and receive services from health plans participating in state health insurance exchanges if they otherwise qualify for such coverage.
- Individuals pending dispositions who satisfy bail requirements and are released into the community will be eligible to enroll in Medicaid and receive services so long as they meet the program requirements.

- Individuals who are pending disposition and remain in jail because they are unable to meet bail conditions may enroll in Medicaid if they satisfy the program requirements but will be ineligible to receive Medicaid services.

Workshop participants discussed the value of eliminating the restriction imposed in the third category. Even if the restriction were maintained, simply ceasing to disenroll the incarcerated from Medicaid could have a substantial impact on continuity of care for them upon release to society.

Further discussion addressed the imperative of facilitating enrollment, particularly among the large and fluid population moving through jails. Jails are viewed as a particularly valuable point of contact for both inmates and their families. Jails might also be able to facilitate the process of enrollment, which can be cumbersome and even overwhelming for a low-resource population. Some inmates and their families have been hampered by low literacy as they attempt to complete paperwork. They often lack essential documentation (government-issued identification, recent paystubs, or bank statements). Homelessness or unstable housing can interfere with communication from the Social Security Administration. Jails may also be in contact with persons who would otherwise avoid interacting with officials—due, for example, to unpaid child support or immigration status. If jail staff made an effort to enroll inmates, this could make a substantial difference to realizing the potential of ACA to provide access to healthcare for uninsured individuals and open reimbursement streams for the localities providing care to inmates, arguably improving equity and health while lowering both health costs and recidivism. This also applies to visiting family members who may be just as vulnerable and underinsured and could benefit from enrollment into health insurance plans under the ACA as well. As Steven Rosenberg affirmed, "Getting people enrolled is the first issue in terms of leveraging the implications of ACA."

WORKFORCE

The workshop also explored implications of the ACA for expanding, improving, and funding the health-related workforce interacting with inmates. Discussion reflected changes in the workforce needed in order to address the needs of inmates. This included not only professional medical care providers, but a range of other actors, such as skilled screeners to work in prisons and jails to screen inmates at intake for mental illness and substance abuse, dementia and age-related disease and disabilities, reproductive health and sexually transmitted infections, health and insurance status of family members, and a range of other issues. For meeting the needs of those on probation and parole, correctional staff trained in cognitive behavioral management and motivational techniques was also discussed. The handling of release and re-entry would also entail a capable workforce to improve continuity of care, ongoing medication and treatment, and enrollment of families in health plans or Medicaid. In particular, this might include community health workers with incarceration experience to help those recently released navigate the complexities of accessing social services and manage their healthcare in the risky period of re-entry. If these services were provided to those newly enrolled under the ACA, would any of these screeners, corrections staff, or community health workers be able to bill their services to Medicaid? Several participants explicitly wondered whether expansion of coverage under ACA would make this possible. If so, Osher commented, "We may have funding streams available within the community that can pick up the slack that historically has increased the budgetary pressure on our correction environments."

QUALITY OF CARE AND ACCOUNTABILITY

The ACA could also conceivably have an impact on the quality of care that medical professionals provide to inmates, particularly if doctors are encouraged or required to participate in accountable care organizations. At present, several workshop participants observed, doctors providing care within correctional facilities are often isolated, practicing in "islands" separated from their peers providing care in the community. As such, they become susceptible to the "culture of fear and cynicism" that was identified as characterizing many correctional environments. Further, their professionalism is unsupported and may atrophy. If practicing outside of health plans or Medicaid, they may also be missed by metrics used to measure and evaluate performance.

All of these might be addressed as the ACA is implemented, with more inmates participating in health plans and Medicaid. This could result in individuals seeing their regular healthcare providers, whether inside or outside correctional facilities. Scott Allen referred to this continuity as the "ideal." Josiah Rich (Department of Medicine and Epidemiology, Warren Alpert Medical School of Brown University, and the Center for Prisoner Health and Human Rights at the Miriam Hospital Immunology Center,) concurred from his own experience providing care, noting that "just seeing a familiar face" improves the experience for both doctor and patient, bolstering trust.

Furthermore, if seeing patients enrolled in Medicaid (whether post-release, on parole or probation, or even during incarceration if the restrictions are changed), then doctors would become "part of the metric,"

Allen explained, and healthcare provided in correctional facilities would no longer be "carved out" of performance and outcome measures. This is also the case for inmates on health plans. Rosenberg observed, "By maintaining coverage for individuals within their health plans while they are within a correctional environment, the health plan's measurements will include the outcome measures." This could help improve the quality of care provided to inmates. Robert Greifinger suggested using the ACA as "leverage to encourage the participation of correctional health professionals in accountable care organizations, which will increase their contact with community healthcare folks." Allen affirmed the potential for improved quality of care when healthcare providers within correctional facilities are "answerable to the community standard."

STATES AND HEALTH PLANS

How much of the potential impact of the ACA is realized will depend in part on how states respond to the law and what initiatives they take to implement it, as well as on the strategies and practices of private health plans. States have recently decided whether to create their own health exchanges (the formal structure through which residents will choose among available plans), coordinate with a health exchange established by the federal government, or opt out and allow residents to utilize the federal health exchange. State choices may influence the effort they put into enrolling inmates, coordinating with Medicaid to make benefits available, and incentivizing health plans to provide care to this population.

In Rich's view, "You can have all the Medicaid you want, but if there isn't a doctor who will see you, or if insurance plans are running away from you," then what good is such coverage? Rosenberg expressed the concern that health plans would shun the inmate population as "a tough reach," and suggested that health plans' "general attitude is 'we don't know anything about caring for this population, and where do we hide?'" The potential for cost savings may help motivate states to implement ACA fully and encourage the participation of health plans.

COST SHIFTS, SAVINGS, AND RECIDIVISM

Greifinger noted that as the federal government will fully subsidize states for the cost of new Medicaid enrollees for the first three years, this will constitute a considerable cost shift away from state and local governments to the federal government. Although incarcerated individuals will still not be eligible to receive Medicaid benefits as the law is currently written, many others involved in the correctional system—including those pending disposition in the community, those on probation and parole, on home confinement, or released, and the families of all these individuals—could access benefits. "That's one of the many reasons I think that state and county criminal justice policy people should be paying attention," Greifinger observed. "There will be a favorable shift from the perspective of the states and the counties."

Rosenberg shared the results of research conducted in the state of Washington (which expends some of its own general fund dollars to provide substance abuse services) that indicates that treating substance abuse results in a decline in arrest rates of between 16 and 33 percent. The overall cost of healthcare to the impacted population also declined. Rosenberg asserted that while the full fiscal and correctional impact of the ACA cannot be predicted, this research suggests if its enactment makes more funds available for substance abuse treatment, the impact could be substantial on both costs and recidivism.

EQUITY AND RIGHTS

By improving access to healthcare for those transitioning out of the criminal justice system, might the ACA also help redress some of the racial and socioeconomic disparities in health and healthcare? When this question was posed, Rosenberg offered a pessimistic answer for the near term. In his assessment, because states face so many challenges in implementing the new law, actions that will improve care specifically for inmates will probably be a low priority. "From where we sit," Rosenberg offered, "this is a promise that ACA could fulfill," but based on his monitoring of state actions thus far, "we're not seeing it yet."

Rosenberg did, however, suggest a provocative route to eventually fulfilling that promise. In prisons, he noted, "Currently, if I'm an offender the sole right I have to care is covered by my constitutional right under the Eighth Amendment as interpreted by the Supreme Court in *Estelle v. Gamble*. On January 1, 2014, if I'm a member of an exchange, I have another right, I have a contractual right between me and the exchange for care. All of a sudden, a different set of rights enters into this." Rosenberg foresees considerable effort on the part of lawyers to determine just how such rights will be exercised. Debates will no doubt address whether the current restriction against receiving Medicaid benefits while incarcerated is maintained, and may also be shaped by whether healthcare providers are employees of the state or of private health plans. Foreseeing an "interesting dynamic," Rosenberg suggested that "the implicit contractual right of the ACA may create some significant changes; we just don't know what they're going to look like yet."

Closing

As the discussion continued, several participants reflected on the relationship between incarceration policies and various aspects of public safety. Several challenged the use of the term as a cover for a moral or political agenda—or confusion. Josiah Rich puzzled that "we as a nation haven't really resolved why we're locking people up. We're not clear about that. Are we rehabilitating, or are we punishing them, or are we doing both?" Jamie Fellner argued, "there is a role for retribution and punishment in a criminal justice system," but that the current rates of incarceration and lengths of sentences go "far beyond legitimate penological goals either of retribution or of incapacitation or of deterrence." Marc Mauer (The Sentencing Project) concurred, "There's something fundamentally off when the wealthiest society in the world maintains the world's largest prison population." Mauer stated that many now believe the United States incarcerates far too many people and keeps them incarcerated for far too long—beyond the point of providing public safety, and at significant opportunity cost to other methods of promoting both public safety and public health.

In practical terms, Faye Taxman pointed out that incarceration has lost its deterrent effect exactly because it has become so widespread. The criminological and sociological literature confirms that, because of current rates, incarceration has "become more normalized in the general population," thus diminishing its value for public safety. Rich also suggested that regardless of moral perspective, a practical assessment of the current system reveals its ineffectiveness in serving public safety. Referring to the mentally ill who are so disproportionately represented in the inmate population, Rich observed a pattern of "somebody incarcerated, and then come[s] back, and then incarcerated again, and then come[s] back, and then incarcerated again. Something's wrong." Rich proposed an outlook "instead of trying to punish people for punishment's sake, let's try and look at it as what are the outcomes we want" because the current system "doesn't make sense if you want public safety."

Mauer also affirmed, "In terms of public safety, we're well past the point of diminishing returns in terms of what we get out of high rates of incarceration." He further emphasized that the choice "is not building prisons or doing nothing" but rather using resources in a variety of other ways to promote public safety. This would involve a "fundamental shift in approach," beginning with a substantial reduction in the prison population overall. Mauer referred to "credible scenarios and policy analysis that suggest a reduction of 50 percent or so in the prison population would not have adverse effects on public safety and would be eminently doable if we have the political will." Mauer cited ongoing efforts in California, New Jersey, and New York, through either policy initiatives or court orders, to produce substantial reductions in prison populations. Learning from these experiences will help guide subsequent efforts. Ceasing the current overinvestment in incarceration, making a 50 percent reduction in the prison population, will permit resources to be redirected toward disadvantaged communities, allowing "justice reinvestments" to redress health and socioeconomic disparities. Mauer acknowledged this is a "challenging shift both politically and practically to make. It seems like the time is ripe to start thinking about how we go about making that shift and what that would look like, and what outcomes we might expect to see."

Bruce Western brought the workshop to a close, articulating several insights that had emerged over the course of discussion. He began by acknowledging that the growth of the incarcerated population in recent decades is partly "in response to a very substantial public health problem." Essentially, he observed, "we wound up to an important degree punishing illness and poverty." Thus, the issues of public health and public safety are deeply intertwined.

Western went on to describe prisons and jails as "Janus-faced institutions." They perpetuate social damage even as they simultaneously deliver much-needed treatment. Thus, "there's a deep paradox in the character of these institutions that we have to come to grips with." To do so, Western proposed a "virtuous circle" in which correctional facilities are actively involved in improving public health and the resulting gains in public health reduce prison populations. How could such a virtuous circle be generated and sustained? Western identified three ideas emerging from the workshop discussion.

First, he noted, the logic of treatment is fundamentally different from the logic of custody, especially as "there is a significant suspension of moral judgment about the status of the patient compared to moral judgment about the status of the prison inmate." Promoting the logic of treatment could help foster the virtuous circle.

Second, Western commented on the depth of the discussion regarding the ethical and political responsibilities of the healthcare community itself (see the section titled "Healthcare Providers" earlier in this report). Acknowledging that he had become far more cognizant of this issue because of the workshop, Western suggested that deeper civic and political engagement on the part of healthcare providers could have tremendous impact on establishing and maximizing the virtuous circle he described.

Finally, Western emphasized the value of making transparent the impact of public health on public safety, broadly conceived. If the link between the two were more widely perceived, this would help sustain the virtuous circle, improving both health and safety.

Bibliography

Adhalt, C., Binswanger, I.A., Steinman, M., Tulsky, J., and Williams, B.A. (2011). Confined to ignorance: The absence of prisoner information from nationally representative health data sets. *Journal of General Internal Medicine, 27*(2), 160-166.

Allen, S., Wakeman, S., Cohen, L., and Rich, J. (2010). Physicians in U.S. prisons in the era of mass incarceration. *International Journal of Prison Health, 6*(3), 100-106.

Andrews, D.A. (2006). Enhancing adherence to risk-need-reponsivity: Making quality a matter of policy. *Criminology and Public Policy, 5,* 595-602.

Andrews, D.A., and Bonta, J. (2006). *The Psychology of Criminal Conduct* (4th ed). Newark, NJ: LexisNexis/Matthew Bender.

Baillargeon, J., Giordano, T.P., Harzke, A.J., Baillargeon, G., Rich, J.D., and Paar, D.P. (2010). Enrollment in outpatient care among newly released prison inmates with HIV infection. *Public Health Reports, 125*(Supplement 1), 64-71.

Baillargeon, J., Hoge, S.K., and Penn, J.V. (2010). Addressing the challenge of community reentry among released inmates with serious mental illness. *American Journal of Community Psychology, 46*(3-4), 361-375.

Beck, A., Harrison, P., Berzofsky, M., Caspar, R., and Krebs, C. (2010). *Sexual Victimization in Prisons and Jails Reported by Inmates, 2008-09*. Washington, DC: U.S. Department of Justice, Bureau of Justice Statistics.

Beckwith, C.G., Zaller, N.D., Fu, J.J., Montague, B.T., and Rich, J.D. (2010). Opportunities to diagnose, treat, and prevent HIV in the criminal justice system. *Journal of Acquired Immune Deficiency Syndromes, 55*(Supplement 1), S49-S55.

Belenko, S., and Peugh, J. (2005). Estimating drug treatment needs among state prison inmates. *Drug and Alcohol Dependence, 77*(3), 269-281.

Binswanger, I.A., Stern, M.F., Deyo, R.A., Heagerty, P.J., Cheadle, A., Elmore, J.G., et al. (2007). Release from prison—A high risk of death for former inmates. *New England Journal of Medicine, 356*(2), 157-165.

Binswanger, I.A., Krueger, P.M., and Steiner, J.F. (2009). **Prevalence of chronic medical conditions among jail and prison inmates in the U.S.A. compared with the general population.** *Journal of Epidemiology and Community Health, 63*(11), 912-919.

Binswanger, I.A., Merrill, J.O., Krueger, P.M., White, M.C., Booth, R.E., and Elmore, J.G. (2010). Gender differences in chronic medical, psychiatric, and substance-dependence disorders among jail inmates. *American Journal of Public Health, 100*(3), 476-482.

Binswanger, I.A., Redmond, N., Steiner, J.F., and Hicks, L.S. (2012). Health disparities and the criminal justice system: An agenda for further research and action. *Journal of Urban Health, 89*(1), 98-107.

Blankenship, K.M., Smoyer, A.B., Bray, S.J., and Mattocks, K. (2005). Black-white disparities in HIV/AIDS: The role of drug policy and the corrections system. *Journal of Health Care for the Poor and Underserved, 16*(4 Supplement B), 140-156.

Booker, C.A., Flygare, C.T., Solomon, L., Ball, S.W., Pustell, M.R., Bazerman, L.B., Simon-Levine, D., Teixeira, P.A., Cruzado-Quinones, J., Kling, R.N., et al. (2012). Linkage to HIV care for jail detainees: Findings from detention to the first 30 days after release. *AIDS and Behavior*, Dec. 6. Available: http://link.springer.com/article/10.1007%2Fs10461-012-0354-3#page-1 [June 2013].

Boutwell, A.E., Allen, S.A., and Rich, J.D. (2005). Opportunities to address the hepatitis C epidemic in the correctional setting. *Clinical Infectious Diseases, 40*(Supplement 5), S367-S372.

Broad, J., Cox, T., Rodriguez, S., Mansour, M., Mennella, C., Murphy-Swallow, D., et al. (2009). The impact of discontinuation of male STD screening services at a large urban county jail: Chicago, 2002-2004. *Sexually Transmitted Diseases, 36*(2 Supplement), S49-S52.

Bureau of Justice Statistics. (2012). *PREA Data Collection Activities, 2012*. Washington, DC: U.S. Department of Justice.

Carson, A., and Sabol, W. (2012). *Correctional Populations in the United States, 2011*. NCJ #239972. Washington, DC: U.S. Department of Justice, Bureau of Justice Statistics. Available: http://bjs.ojp.usdoj.gov/content/pub/pdf/cpus11.pdf [Feb. 2013].

Chandler, R.K., Fletcher, B.W., and Volkow, N.D. (2009). Treating drug abuse and addiction in the criminal justice system: Improving public health and safety. *Journal of the American Medical Association, 301*(2), 183-190.

Clarke, J.G., and Waring, M.E. (2012). Overweight, obesity, and weight change among incarcerated women. *Journal of Correctional Health Care, 18*(4), 4285-4292.

Damberg, C.L., Shaw, R., Teleki, S.S., Hiatt, L., and Asch, S.M. (2011). A review of quality measures used by state and federal prisons. *Journal of Correctional Health Care, 17*(2), 122-137.

Desai, A.A., Latta, E.T., Spaulding, A., Rich, J.D., and Flanigan, T.P. (2002). The importance of routine HIV testing in the incarcerated population: The Rhode Island experience. *AIDS Education and Prevention, 14*(5 Supplement B), 45-52.

Ditton, P.M. (1999). *Mental Health and Treatment of Inmates and Probationers*. NCJ #174463. Washington, DC: U.S. Department of Justice, Bureau of Justice Statistics. Available: http://www.bjs.gov/content/pub/pdf/mhtip.pdf [May 2013].

Draine, J., Ahuja, D., Altice, F.L., Arriola, K.J., Avery, A.K., Beckwith, C.G., et al. (2011). Strategies to enhance linkages between care for HIV/AIDS in jail and community settings. *AIDS Care, 23*(3), 366-377.

Fazel, S., and Danesh, J. (2002). Serious mental disorder in 23000 prisoners: A systematic review of 62 surveys. *Lancet, 359*(9306), 545-550.

Fazel, S., Bains, P., and Doll, H. (2006). Substance abuse and dependence in prisoners: A systematic review. *Addiction, 101*(2), 181-191.

Federal Bureau of Prisons. (2008). *The Federal Bureau of Prison's Efforts to Manage Inmate Health Care*. Washington, DC: U.S. Department of Justice, Office of the Inspector General.

Fellner, J. (2006). A correctional quandary: Mental illness and prison rules. *Harvard Civil Rights and Civil Liberties Law Review, 41*, 391-412.

Fellner, J. (2007). Policy and the prevalence of mental illness in U.S. prisons. *Correctional Mental Health Report, 8*(5), 67-71.

Fellner, J. (2012). *Old Behind Bars: The Aging Prison Population in the United States*. New York: Human Rights Watch. Available: http://www.hrw.org/sites/default/files/reports/usprisons0112webwcover_0.pdf [May 2013].

Fellner, J., and Abramsky, S. (2003). *Ill-Equipped: U.S. Prisons and Offenders with Mental Illness*. New York: Human Rights Watch. Available: http://www.hrw.org/reports/2003/usa1003/usa1003.pdf [May 2013].

Fisher, A.A., and Hatton, D.C. (2010). A study of women prisoners' use of co-payments for healthcare: Issues of access. *Women's Health Issues, 20*(3), 185-192.

Fontana, L., and Beckerman, A. (2007). Recently released with HIV/AIDS: Primary care treatment needs and experiences. *Journal of Health Care for the Poor and Underserved, 18*(3), 699-714.

Glaze, L.E. (2010). *Correctional Populations in the United States, 2009*. Washington, DC: U.S. Department of Justice, Bureau of Justice Statistics. Available: http://www.bjs.gov/content/pub/pdf/cpus09.pdf [May 2013].

Gough, E., Kempf, M.C., Graham, L., Manzanero, M., Hook, E.W., Bartolucci, A., et al. (2010). HIV and hepatitis B and C incidence rates in U.S. correctional populations and high-risk groups: A systematic review and meta-analysis. *BMC Public Health, 10*, 777.

Greifinger, R.B. (2007). Thirty years since *Estelle v. Gamble*. In R.B. Greifinger (Ed.), *Public Health Behind Bars: From Prisons to Communities* (pp. 4-8). New York: Springer.

Hammett, T.M. (2006). HIV/AIDS and other infectious diseases among correctional inmates: Transmission, burden, and an appropriate response. *American Journal of Public Health, 96*(6), 974-978.

Haney, C. (2003). Mental health issues in long-term solitary and "Supermax" confinement. *Crime & Delinquency, 49*(1), 124-156.

Harzke, A.J., Baillargeon, J.G., Pruitt, S.L., Pulvino, J.S., Paar, D.P., and Kelley, M.F. (2010). Prevalence of chronic medical conditions among inmates in the Texas prison system. *Journal of Urban Health, 87*(3), 486-503.

Howard, D.L., Strobino, D., Sherman, S.G., and Crum, R.M. (2009). Timing of incarceration during pregnancy and birth outcomes: Exploring racial differences. *Maternal and Child Health Journal, 13*(4), 457-466.

Humphreys, K. (2012). Federal policy on criminal offenders who have substance use disorders: How can we maximize public health and public safety? *Substance Abuse, 33*(1), 5-8.

James, D.J. (2004). *Profile of Jail Inmates, 2002*. NCJ #201932. Washington, DC: U.S. Department of Justice, Bureau of Justice Statistics. Available: http://bjs.ojp.usdoj.gov/content/pub/pdf/pji02.pdf [Feb. 2013].

James, D.J., and Glaze, L.E. (2006). *Mental Health Problems of Prison and Jail Inmates*. Washington, DC: U.S. Department of Justice, Bureau of Justice Statistics.

Jenness, V., Maxson, C., Sumner, J., and Matsuda, K. (2010). Accomplishing the difficult but not impossible: Collecting self-report data on inmate-on-inmate sexual assault in prison. *Criminal Justice Law Review, 21*(1), 3-30.

Karberg, J., and James, D. (2005). *Substance Dependence, Abuse, and Treatment of Jail Inmates, 2002*. Washington, DC: U.S. Department of Justice, Bureau of Justice Statistics.

Kauffman, R.M., Ferketich, A.K., Murray, D.M., Bellair, P.E., and Wewers, M.E. (2011). Tobacco use by male prisoners under an indoor smoking ban. *Nicotine & Tobacco Research, 13*(6), 449-456.

Kendig, N.E. (2004). Correctional health care systems and collaboration with academic medicine. *Journal of the American Medical Association, 292*(4), 501-503.

Kessler, R.C., Nelson, C.B., McGonagle, K.A., Edlund, M.J., Frank, R.G., and Leaf, P.J. (1996). The epidemiology of co-occurring addictive and mental disorders: Implications for prevention and service utilization. *American Journal of Orthopsychiatry, 66*(1), 17-31.

Larney, S., Kopinski, H., Beckwith, C., Zaller, N., Des Jarlais, D., Hagan, H., et al. (2013). The incidence and prevalence of hepatitis C in prisons and other closed settings: Results of a systematic review and meta-analysis. *Hepatology,* doi: 10.1002/hep.26387. Available: http://onlinelibrary.wiley.com/doi/10.1002/hep.26387/pdf [June 2013].

Latessa, E.J. (2012). *What Works and What Doesn't in Reducing Recidivism: Applying the Principles of Effective Intervention to Offender Reentry.* Presentation at the Center for Criminal Justice Research, School of Criminal Justice, University of Cincinnati, Ohio.

Lee, H., and Wildeman, C. (2013). Things fall apart: Health consequences of mass imprisonment for African American women. *Review of Black Political Economy, 30,* 39-52. Available: http://link.springer.com/content/pdf/10.1007/s12114-011-9112-4.pdf [June 2013].

Lewis, C. (2006). Treating incarcerated women: Gender matters. *Psychiatric Clinics of North America, 29*(3), 773-789.

Lincoln, T., Kennedy, S., Tuthill, R., Roberts, C., Conklin, T.J., and Hammett, T.M. (2006). Facilitators and barriers to continuing healthcare after jail: A community-integrated program. *Journal of Ambulatory Care Management, 29*(1), 2-16.

London, A., and Myers, N. (2006). Race, incarceration, and health: A life-course approach. *Research on Aging, 28*(3), 409-422.

Macalino, G.E., Dhawan, D., and Rich, J.D. (2005). A missed opportunity: Hepatitis C screening of prisoners. *American Journal of Public Health, 95*(10), 1739-1740.

Maguire, K. (Ed.) (2011) *Sourcebook of Criminal Justice Statistics.* Albany, NY: University at Albany, Hindelang Criminal Justice Research Center, Tables 6.13 and 6.28. Available: http://www.albany.edu/sourcebook [May 2013].

Marlow, E., White, M.C., and Chesla, C.A. (2010). Barriers and facilitators: Parolees' perceptions of community health care. *Journal of Correctional Health Care, 16*(1), 17-26.

Maruschak, L.M. (2012). *HIV in Prisons 2001-2010.* Washington, DC: U.S. Department of Justice, Bureau of Justice Statistics.

McCarty, D., and Chandler, R.K. (2009). Understanding the importance of organizational and system variables on addiction treatment services within criminal justice settings. *Drug and Alcohol Dependency, 103*(Supplement 1), S91-S93.

Mears, D., Winterfield, L., Hunsaker, J., Moore, G., and White, R. (2002). *Drug Treatment in the Criminal Justice System: The Current State of Knowledge.* Washington, DC: The Urban Institute.

Mellow, J., and Greifinger, R.B. (2007). Successful reentry: The perspective of private correctional health care providers. *Journal of Urban Health, 84*(1), 85-98.

Metzner, J.L., and Fellner, J. (2010). Solitary confinement and mental illness in U.S. prisons: A challenge for medical ethics. *Journal of the American Academy of Psychiatry and the Law, 38*(1), 104-108.

Minton, T. (2012). *Jail Inmates at Mid-year 2011, Statistical Tables.* NCJ #237961. Washington, DC: U.S. Department of Justice, Bureau of Justice Statistics. Available: http://bjs.ojp.usdoj.gov/content/pub/pdf/jim11st.pdf [Feb. 2013].

Moller, L. (2007). *Health in Prisons: A WHO Guide to the Essentials in Prison Health.* Geneva, Switzerland: World Health Organization.

Moloney, K.P., van den Bergh, B.J., and Moller, L.F. (2009). Women in prison: The central issues of gender characteristics and trauma history. *Public Health, 123*(6), 426-430.

Montague, B.T., Rosen, D.L., Solomon, L., Nunn, A., Green, T., Costa, M., et al. (2012). Tracking linkage to HIV care for former prisoners: A public health priority. *Virulence, 3*(3), 319-324.

Morabito, M.S. (2007). Horizons of context: Understanding the police decision to arrest people with mental illness. *Psychiatric Services, 58*(12), 1582-1587.

Mumola, C., and Karberg, J. (2006). *Drug Use and Dependence, State and Federal Prisoners, 2004.* Washington, DC: U.S. Department of Justice, Bureau of Justice Statistics.

Murray, J., Farrington, D.P., and Sekol, I. (2012). Children's antisocial behavior, mental health, drug use, and educational performance after parental incarceration: A systematic review and meta-analysis. *Psychological Bulletin, 138*(2), 175-210.

National Commission on Correctional Health Care. (2002). *The Health Status of Soon-to-Be-Released Inmates: A Report to Congress.* Chicago, IL: National Commission on Correctional Health Care.

Nijhawan, A.E., Salloway, R., Nunn, A.S., Poshkus, M., and Clarke, J.G. (2010). Preventive healthcare for underserved women: Results of a prison survey. *Journal of Women's Health, 19*(1), 17-22.

Nordstrom, B.R., and Williams, A.R. (2012). Drug treatments in criminal justice settings. *Psychiatric Clinics of North America, 35*(2), 375-391.

Nunn, A., Zaller, N., Dickman, S., Trimbur, C., Nijhawan, A., and Rich, J.D. (2009). Methadone and buprenorphine prescribing and referral practices in U.S. prison systems: Results from a nationwide survey. *Drug and Alcohol Dependency, 105*(1-2), 83-88.

Nunn, A., Cornwall, A., Fu, J., Bazerman, L., Loewenthal, H., and Beckwith, C. (2010). Linking HIV-positive jail inmates to treatment, care, and social services after release: Results from a qualitative assessment of the COMPASS Program. *Journal of Urban Health, 87*(6), 954-968.

Oser, C.B., Knudsen, H.K., Staton-Tindall, M., Taxman, F., and Leukefeld, C. (2009). Organizational-level correlates of the provision of detoxification services and medication-based treatments for substance abuse in correctional institutions. *Drug and Alcohol Dependency, 103*(Supplement 1), S73-S81.

Phillips, S. (2012). *The Affordable Care Act: Implications for Public Safety and Corrections Populations.* Washington, DC: The Sentencing Project.

Regenstein, M., and Christie-Maples, J. (2012). *Medicaid Coverage for Individuals in Jail Pending Disposition: Opportunities for Improved Health and Health Care at Lower Costs.* Washington, DC: Department of Public Health Policy, School of Public Health and Health Service, George Washington University. Available: http://sphhs.gwu.edu/departments/healthpolicy/publications/DHP%20Report%20Regenstein%2010%20reasons%20November%206.pdf [April 2012].

Rich, J.D., Holmes, L., Salas, C., Macalino, G., Davis, D., Ryczek, J., and Flanigan, T. (2001). Successful linkage of medical care and community services for HIV-positive offenders being released from prison. *Journal of Urban Health, 78*(2), 279-289.

Rich, J.D., Boutwell, A.E., Shield, D.C., Key, R.G., McKenzie, M., Clarke, J.G., et al. (2005). Attitudes and practices regarding the use of methadone in U.S. state and federal prisons. *Journal of Urban Health, 82*(3), 411-419.

Rich, J.D., Wakeman, S.E., and Dickman, S.L. (2011). Medicine and the epidemic of incarceration in the United States. *New England Journal of Medicine, 364*(22), 2081-2083.

Rich, J.D., Dumont, D., and Allen, S. (2012). *Incarceration and Health.* Working paper prepared for the National Academies Workshop on Health and Incarceration, Dec. 5, Washington, DC. Available: http://sites.nationalacademies.org/DBASSE/CLAJ/DBASSE_083370 [May 2013].

Rosen, D.L., Hammond, W.P., Wohl, D.A., and Golin, C.E. (2012). Disease prevalence and use of health care among a national sample of black and white male state prisoners. *Journal of Health Care for the Poor and Underserved, 23*(1), 254-272.

Schnittker, J., and John, A. (2007). Enduring stigma: The long-term effects of incarceration on health. *Journal of Health and Social Behavior, 48*(2), 115-130.

Spaulding, A.C., Weinbaum, C.M., Lau, D.T., Sterling, R., Seeff, L.B., Margolis, H.S., et al. (2006). A framework for management of hepatitis C in prisons. *Annals of Internal Medicine, 144*(10), 762-769.

Spaulding, A.C., Seals, R.M., Page, M.J., Brzozowski, A.K., Rhodes, W., and Hammett, T.M. (2009). HIV/AIDS among inmates of and releases from U.S. correctional facilities, 2006: Declining share of epidemic but persistent public health opportunity. *PLoS One, 4*(11), e7558.

Steadman, H.J., Osher, F.C., Robbins, P.C., Case, B., and Samuels, S. (2009). Prevalence of serious mental illness among jail inmates. *Psychiatric Services, 60*(6), 761-765.

Substance Abuse and Mental Health Services Administration. (2000). *Substance Abuse Treatment in Adult and Juvenile Correctional Facilities: Findings from the Uniform Facility Data Set 1997 Survey of Correctional Facilities.* Washington, DC: U.S. Department of Health and Human Services, Substance Abuse and Mental Health Services Administration.

Taxman, F.S., Henderson, C.E., and Belenko, S. (2009). Organizational context, systems change, and adopting treatment delivery systems in the criminal justice system. *Drug and Alcohol Dependency, 103*(Supplement 1), S1-S6.

Varan, A., Mercer, D., Stein, M., and Spaulding, A. (2012). *State Prison System Surveillance of Hepatitis C Exposure: Limited Data Show Declining Share of U.S. Epidemic.* Paper presented at the Fifth Academic and Health Policy Conference on Correctional Health, Atlanta, GA.

Wakeman, S.E., McKinney, M.E., and Rich, J.D. (2009). Filling the gap: The importance of Medicaid continuity for former inmates. *Journal of General Internal Medicine, 24*(7), 860-862.

Wang, E.A., and Green, J. (2010). Incarceration as a key variable in racial disparities of asthma prevalence. *BMC Public Health, 10*, 290.

Wang, E.A., White, M.C., Jamison, R., Goldenson, J., Estes, M., and Tulsky, J.P. (2008). Discharge planning and continuity of health care: Findings from the San Francisco County jail. *American Journal of Public Health, 98*(12), 2182-2184.

Wang, E.A., Pletcher, M., Lin, F., Vittinghoff, E., Kertesz, S.G., Kiefe, C.I., et al. (2009). Incarceration, incident hypertension, and access to health care: Findings from the coronary artery risk development in young adults (CARDIA) study. *Archives of Internal Medicine, 169*(7), 687-693.

Wildeman, C. (2012). Imprisonment and (inequality in) population health. *Social Science Research, 41*, 74-91.

Wildeman, C., and Muller, C. (2012). Mass imprisonment and inequality in health and family life. *Annual Review of Law and Social Science, 8*, 11-30.

Wildeman, C., Schnittker, J., and Turney, K. (2012). Despair by association? The mental health of mothers with children by recently incarcerated fathers. *American Sociological Review, 77*, 216-243.

Williams, B.A., and Abraldes, R. (2010). Growing older: Challenges of prison and reentry for the aging population. In R.B. Greifinger (Ed.), *Public Health Behind Bars: From Prisons to Communities* (pp. 56-72). New York: Springer.

Williams, B.A., McGuire, J., Lindsay, R.G., Baillargeon, J., Cenzer, I.S., Lee, S.J., and Kushel, M. (2010). Coming home: Health status and homelessness risk of older pre-release prisoners. *Journal of General Internal Medicine, 25*(10), 1038-1044.

Williams, B.A., Sudore, R.L., Greifinger, R., and Morrison, R.S. (2011). Balancing punishment and compassion for seriously ill prisoners. *Annals of Internal Medicine, 155*, 122-126.

Williams, B.A., Goodwin, J.S., Baillargeon, J., Ahalt, C., and Walter, L.C. (2012a). Addressing the aging crisis in U.S. criminal justice healthcare. *Journal of American Geriatric Society, 60*(6), 1150-1156.

Williams, B.A., Stern, M.F., Mellow, J., Safer, M., and Greifinger, R.B. (2012b). Aging in correctional custody: Setting a policy agenda for older prisoner health care. *American Journal of Public Health, 102*(8), 1475-1481.

Wilper, A.P., Woolhandler, S., Boyd, J.W., Lasser, K.E., McCormick, D., Bor, D.H., et al. (2009). The health and health care of U.S. prisoners: Results of a nationwide survey. *American Journal of Public Health, 99*(4), 666-672.

Zaller, N.D., Holmes, L., Dyl, A.C., Mitty, J.A., Beckwith, C.G., Flanigan, T.P., et al. (2008). Linkage to treatment and supportive services among HIV-positive ex-offenders in Project Bridge. *Journal of Health Care for the Poor and Underserved, 19*(2), 522-531.

Appendix

Workshop Agenda and Participants

The rate of incarceration in the United States is very high both historically and in comparison to that of other developed nations. Those in or entering U.S. jails and prisons experience symptoms of drug dependence or abuse, severe mental illness, HIV infection, diabetes mellitus, and other chronic medical conditions at far higher rates than the general population. This is a problem not just for them but for the communities from which they come and to which, in nearly all cases, they will return.

To explore and expand the knowledge basis for policies to address the health needs of those in prison and benefit them and their home communities, a public workshop will bring together leading academic and practicing experts, to summarize what is known about these issues, what critical gaps in our knowledge should be filled with new research, and what appear to be the best opportunities to improve healthcare for those who are now or will be incarcerated. The half-day workshop will be held at the National Academy of Sciences' (NAS') Keck Center, Room 110, 500 5th Street NW, Washington, DC, from 12:30 to 4:30 p.m., on Wednesday, December 5, 2012.

This workshop is jointly sponsored by the Institute of Medicine's Board on the Health of Select Populations and the National Research Council's (NRC's) Committee on Law and Justice. Its products will inform a current study by an ad hoc committee of the NRC on causes, consequences, and alternatives to high rates of incarceration in the United States.

Presentations and discussion will address one or more of the following questions:

1. What can we say with confidence about the incidence and sources of major health problems among the population subject to incarceration? What are the critical gaps in our knowledge of these questions?
2. What is the status and range of variation in the quality of care, including screening and treatment, provided upon incarceration, while in jail or prison, and linkage to care upon release? What are the characteristics of high-performing systems (i.e., best practices) providing screening and care to prisoners, coordinating access to care during and following incarceration, and transferring medical information and records to and from other medical care providers? How are these related empirically to the health of prisoners and communities with a high incidence of incarceration and release?
3. What is and what determines the impact of incarceration and release on the health of populations where incarceration and release are concentrated? What are their effects on racial or ethnic disparities in healthcare and health?
4. From a public health standpoint, what are the best opportunities for improving both the health of those in prisons and jails and the health risks they present when released? How can implementation of the Affordable Care Act ensure continuity of medical care for those released from prison? What existing programs at the federal, state, and local/community levels are novel and evidence promise of reducing morbidity among prisoners and ensuring continuity of care following release?
5. What promising innovative outreach and engagement models exist such as successfully employing prisoners or former prisoners in peer health education and/or in caretaker programs directed toward elderly/disabled prisoners and those with substance abuse histories?

Invited participants include

Bruce Western, Harvard University*
Josiah Rich, M.D., Warren Alpert Medical School of Brown University*
Craig Haney, University of California, Santa Cruz*

---

*Indicates a member of the National Research Council and Institute of Medicine Committee on Causes and Consequences of High Rates of Incarceration.

Scott Allen, University of California, Riverside
Redonna Chandler, National Institute on Drug Abuse
Jennifer Clarke, M.D., Brown University Medical Center
Jamie Fellner, Human Rights Watch
Robert Greifinger, M.D., John Jay College of Criminal Justice, City University of New York
Newton Kendig, M.D., Federal Bureau of Prisons
Marc Mauer, The Sentencing Project
Fred Osher, M.D., Council of State Governments
Steven Rosenberg, Community Oriented Correctional Health Services
Faye Taxman, George Mason University
Emily Wang, M.D., Yale University
Chris Wildeman, Yale University
Brie Williams, M.D., University of California, San Francisco

The workshop will be in a roundtable format. Brief presentations will be followed by questions and discussion organized to address the questions posed above.

AGENDA

12:30 p.m. **Welcome, Plan for the Afternoon, and Overview**
Moderating:
Josiah Rich, Committee on Causes and Consequences of High Rates of Incarceration

1:00 p.m. **Incidence and Sources of Health Problems of the Population Subject to Incarceration**
Discussants:
Scott Allen, University of California, Riverside
Jennifer Clarke, Brown University Medical Center
Emily Wang, Yale University
Brie Williams, University of California, San Francisco

1:45 p.m. **Care, Screening, and Treatment in Prison and On Release**
Discussants:
Jamie Fellner, Human Rights Watch
Craig Haney, University of California, Santa Cruz
Newton Kendig, Federal Bureau of Prisons
Fred Osher, University of Maryland

2:30 p.m. **Public Health Impacts**
Discussants:
Robert Greifinger, John Jay College of Criminal Justice, CUNY
Steven Rosenberg, Community Oriented Correctional Health Services
Christopher Wildeman, Yale University

3:15 p.m. **Opportunities and Models for Improving Health and Reducing Health Risks—Innovative Care Models and Evidence of Effects**
Discussants:
Redonna Chandler, National Institute on Drug Abuse
Marc Mauer, The Sentencing Project
Faye Taxman, George Mason University

4:00 p.m. **General Discussion and Conclusions**
Bruce Western and Josiah Rich

4:30 p.m. **Adjourn**